CEOs and Business Leaders

Leading with Emotional Courage is a trailblazing idea, inspirational manifesto and eminently achievable manual. Peter Bregman's central idea, "if you can feel everything, you can do anything," instantly became my motto for forging more productive and rewarding relationships in every aspect of my life. It's ingenious, it's intuitive, and it works.

Jeffrey Seller, Four time Tony Award winning producer of *Hamilton, Rent, Avenue Q, In the Heights*.

Leading with Emotional Courage is a terrific guide that explains why and how we need to look inward before we can drive leadership forward. It will also help you connect on a deeper level with those around you—an absolute necessity if you want to get your most important work done.

James A. Forese, President, Citigroup

Peter is a master storyteller who offers compelling and important takeaways that really do make a difference. The principles in this book are the ones I believe in, and they are aligned with those that helped me and my tribe build a culture that resulted in a 93% employee engagement level at WD-40 Company.

Garry Ridge – CEO WD-40 Company & coauthor with Ken Blanchard – *Helping People Win at Work*

We must see ourselves 'life size,' as Peter Drucker instructed. *Leading with Emotional Courage* is a leader's blueprint to do so.

Frances Hesselbein, Chairman, The Frances Hesselbein Leadership Forum, Former CEO of the Girl Scouts, and Presidential Medal of Freedom recipient

Becoming a Values-based leader requires you to first be capable of leading yourself. Peter does a fantastic job of demonstrating why emotional courage is absolutely key to your personal leadership journey. I learned a lot by reading Peter's book.

Harry Kraemer, Jr, Professor, Northwestern Kellogg School of Mgmt; Former Chairman and CEO, BAXTER International

After reading this book, you will want to share it with your colleagues, your kids, and others in your life. Peter is a master at drawing readers in with self-evaluation, compelling stories, and concrete take-aways. This book will stay on my bookshelf as a reference.

Asheesh Advani, CEO, JA (Junior Achievement) Worldwide

Leading with Emotional Courage is good for business, good for people, and good for the planet. Bregman's book offers the communications tools environmentalists and other nonprofit leaders need to transform tough conversations into progress and action.

Mark R. Tercek, President and CEO of The Nature Conservancy

Leading with Emotional Courage brilliantly identifies the often unnoticed emotional undercurrents of high-stakes business situations and the dynamics of everyday interactions. By making conscious the unconscious, this book offers us control over our own decisions and actions, asking us to open our minds and be curious when emotions are provoked. It has helped me personally to turn some of my most counter-productive reactions into questions. With practical, real-life examples and bite-sized nuggets of information, this book is relevant to everyone, not just ultra-senior leadership.

Michael Thatcher, CEO, Charity Navigator

At the end of the day, Peter gives useful tools for people to own their unique strength and power to be bold leaders in the board room and at the kitchen table

Randall Tucker, Mastercard Chief Inclusion Officer.

Emotional Courage is the foundation for inspirational and effective leadership. Peter Bregman's groundbreaking and timely book, *Leading with Emotional Courage*, does not merely inspire action, it cultivates it. Through concrete and actionable how-to's and compelling stories, this book will change the way you make decisions, how you speak in a boardroom, and actually how you feel at the end of each day. *Leading with Emotional Courage* is right on target and surprisingly different than anything out there. I feel like I've been waiting for this book for a long time!

James M. Citrin, Leader, Spencer Stuart CEO Practice, Author, *You're in Charge, Now What?*

Authors and Thought Leaders

This is a brave and generous book about being brave and generous. Emotional courage isn't about getting what we want, it's about serving others. Peter Bregman is sharing useful magic here.

Seth Godin, author of *Linchpin*

Emotional courage is the courage to *feel*. It's what stands between us and the difficult things we must do as leaders. Emotional courage grows stronger when you practice it—by taking a risk, making a decision, or otherwise following through when you may not be comfortable doing so. It's about getting out of your own way and having the emotional freedom to *act*. Want to know more? Then follow through and read this book!

Ken Blanchard, coauthor of *The New One Minute Manager*® and *Servant Leadership in Action*

Peter's concept of Emotional Courage is a game-changer. It isn't just another theory about productivity or leadership—it's a truth you can feel. It affects every aspect of your leadership and every relationship in your life. The beauty of this book is that it helps you actually strengthen those critical mental-emotional muscles and will make even the most successful leaders better.

Marshall Goldsmith – The author of the #1
New York Times **bestseller** *Triggers*

Leading with Emotional Courage tackles a tough subject that isn't much talked about in the business world: the hard emotions that we all experience. If you courageously adopt the advice in this breakthrough book, you can begin the tough conversations that lead to real change, build more trusting relationships, and perhaps even become an inspiration to others.

Daniel H. Pink, author of *WHEN and DRIVE*

Want to learn how to brave the fears associated with difficult inter-personal exchanges on the job and elsewhere? *Leading with Emotional Courage,* brimming with applicable insights and lessons, is definitely the book for you.

Robert B. Cialdini, author of *Influence*
and Pre-Suasion

Change begins from within; so does leadership. Bregman's insights help leaders gain personal confidence so that they can approach others with a clear purpose and bold, courageous actions. This marvelous book lets me feel like Peter is sitting next to me, coaching me how to be more effective. The insights resonate, the assessments inform, and the stories inspire.

Dave Ulrich, Rensis Likert Professor, Ross School
of Business, University of Michigan
Partner, The RBL Group

It's incredibly refreshing to get this sort of wise and kind advice from someone who specializes in helping leaders get "massive traction". Most voices you'd hear today urging "massive traction" would speak fast, hard, unrelenting exhortations couched in inspirational illustrations of super-human performance. As human-centered-designers, we at the Life Design Lab at Stanford aren't too keen on those driven voices. We're looking to help people be more human – not super-human, which is a very different, and frankly in-human, thing. Peter Bregman has a different voice. What other "massive traction-getting" coaches will suggest that compassion is a critical foundation of self-confidence or that you need to master irrelevancy if you're going to succeed (and better do so well before retirement)? I've been assigning students to read Peter's contrary ideas for years and I recommend this book to you. I finally got to share coffee with him face-to-face and had one of the best first dates of all time. Pull up a chair with this book and share a coffee with Peter. You'll have a lovely time and be better for it.

Dave Evans, Co-Founder, Stanford Life Design Lab, Co-author, NYT #1 Bestseller, *Designing Your Life*, early Apple, co-founder Electronic Arts

Emotional courage is the superpower of the 21st Century! We live in a world where it is far easier to avoid our feelings than it is to feel them. As such, emotional courage is becoming rare at the same time that it is increasingly valuable. The people who cultivate emotional courage—who are confident, connected, and committed to their purpose—will thrive. *Leading with Emotional Courage* is an accessible action plan for breaking through the emotional barriers that prevent people from doing what they want to do.

Christine Carter, PhD, Author of *The Sweet Spot: How to Accomplish More by Doing Less and Raising Happiness*

Engaging and relevant, Peter Bregman's *Leading with Emotional Courage* provides a clear and practical framework to follow when facing emotionally-charged situations. He challenges us to face our fears and stand strong by offering both principles and skills that teach us how to confidently act before being acted upon. A superb read!

Stephen M. R. Covey, The *New York Times* and # 1 *Wall Street Journal* bestselling author of *The Speed of Trust* and coauthor of *Smart Trust*

Leading without courage is not really leading at all. Bregman presents a compelling argument for the power of embracing difficult emotions.

Cal Newport, author of *Deep Work*

Leading with Emotional Courage is about putting your whole self into something. About embracing your fears, expressing your passions, showing your vulnerabilities, and engaging fully with others. It's a book that you do not simply read. Instead, you experience it. It's full of pathos and compassion, enlightenment and practicality. It's like conversing with your best friend. You come away feeling refreshed, entertained, and wiser. Peter Bregman is a master storyteller, and he enlivens his sage counsel with scores of personal tales, joyfully told, each containing simple wisdom and hard truths. There are lots of how-to-do books on the market. *Leading with Emotional Courage* isn't one of them. It's a how-to-be book, and I guarantee you that you'll want to be more like the person Peter describes once you've experienced this book. I highly recommend it.

Jim Kouzes, coauthor of the bestselling *The Leadership Challenge* and the Dean's Executive Fellow of Leadership, Leavey School of Business, Santa Clara University

There's a line between the domineering, overbearing management style of decades past—less effective because it's tone deaf to people—and an increasingly self-aware and people-oriented leadership style that can be less effective if it's too wimpy to get the job done. Bregman offers a thoughtful guide to finding and walking that sometimes elusive line. *Leading with Emotional Courage* offers manageable, bite-sized insights into thought and behavior changes that can help any leader be empathetic enough to honor our shared humanity but still courageous enough to make the tough decisions and initiate the hard conversations essential to a thriving workplace.

Whitney Johnson, Thinkers50 Leading Management Thinker, Critically-acclaimed author of *Disrupt Yourself*

Peter Bregman gives nuanced advice on how we can navigate the complex landscape of our emotional life—to become better leaders, (and better human beings), by being more connected to ourselves and others.

Tal Ben-Shahar, author of *The Joy of Leadership*

To be effective, leaders must move the heart, starting with their own. Bregman brilliantly highlights the often overlooked, but critical aspect of leadership – the courage to feel. Read this book to tap into the power of emotion and unleash your and your team's true potential.

Sanyin Siang, author of *The Launch Book*; **Executive Director, Duke University Fuqua/Coach K Center on Leadership & Ethics**

Emotional Courage is a wonderful reminder that if you are willing to feel everything you can do anything. The book, laced with Bregman's own courageous honesty and openness, will help you build your confidence, bring out the best in others, and summon the emotional courage you need to succeed as a leader.

Liz Wiseman, *New York Times* **bestselling author of** *Multipliers and Rookie Smarts*

In *Leading with Emotional Courage*, Peter Bregman provides us with a novel roadmap for how to embrace, rather than avoid, difficult emotions and, in so doing, live more fulfilling lives. The book is deeply insightful, a pleasure to read, and an indispensable guide for making discomfort and conflict a trusted ally and friend.

Andy Molinsky, Ph.D., author of *Reach and Global Dexterity*

Government and Military Leaders

Cowardice, as characterized by excessive self-interest, has become pervasive across our society. Peter Bregman has given us the tools to be emotionally courageous. As leaders we want to have tough conversations that benefit our organizations, and *Leading with Emotional Courage* shows us the way. Readers will emerge from *Leading with Emotional Courage* with renewed enthusiasm for the day to day challenges of leading. Peter Bregman's book promises to free a huge cohort of leaders from the anxieties that get in the way of doing what's right, instead of what's easy. Choosing the harder right over the easy wrong is one of the "Holy Grails" of leader development—and in *Leading with Emotional Courage*, Peter Bregman has captured that prize. Finally, a book to inspire those of us who lead through the conflict inherent to organizations.

Thomas A. Kolditz, PhD, Brigadier General, US Army (ret), Professor Emeritus, US Military Academy, West Point, Director, Ann & John Doerr Institute for New Leaders, Rice University

Leading with Emotional Courage is a great guide for practitioners who want to heighten their ability to influence others effectively. The book clearly identifies four elements associated with exhibiting emotional courage and provides tangible exercises in service of strengthening one's competence in a given area. I recommend this book to anyone who is committed to becoming a better leader!

Bernie Banks, Brigadier General, US Army (ret), Associate Dean of Leadership Development, Northwestern University's Kellogg School of Management

Peter has spoken with such candor of the interior conversations we use to magnify or sabotage our leadership moments. It's like having a workable path, where you are taught to watch yourself and learn to lead. Take this path; you'll be larger for it.

Charlotte Beers, Former CEO Ogilvy, Former Undersecretary of State

What a lovely mix of personal and professional anecdotes and straight talk about the importance of taking emotions – yours and your colleagues – into account in the task of leading an organization. As Bregman's book so eloquently explains, as long as organizations are composed of humans and not robots, the fundamental challenge of corporate leadership is to get a diverse group of highly emotional creatures to work together effectively – which requires that leaders confront, head on, the need of everyone in the organization to have a sense of common purpose and connectedness. As leaders, we need the emotional courage to engage with our colleagues where they live, where the desire for affirmation and the fear of failure are constantly in play. I am grateful to Peter for writing this book.

Jim Millstein, Founder, Chairman, and Chief Executive Officer of Millstein & Co., Former Chief Restructuring Officer at the U.S. Department of the Treasury

Emotional courage is critical to getting anything important done. And Bregman's book is the essential primer to developing it. If you lead – or aspire to lead – read this book. The world needs more people with emotional courage.

Mark Sanford, Unites States Congressman

LEADING
WITH
EMOTIONAL
COURAGE

PETER BREGMAN

LEADING
WITH
EMOTIONAL
COURAGE

HOW TO HAVE HARD CONVERSATIONS,
CREATE ACCOUNTABILITY, AND INSPIRE ACTION
ON YOUR MOST IMPORTANT WORK

WILEY

Published by John Wiley & Sons, Inc., Hoboken, New Jersey.
Published simultaneously in Canada.

For general information on our other products and services or for technical support, please contact our Customer Care Department within the United States at (800) 762–2974, outside the United States at (317) 572–3993 or fax (317) 572–4002.

Wiley publishes in a variety of print and electronic formats and by print-on-demand. Some material included with standard print versions of this book may not be included in e-books or in print-on-demand. If this book refers to media such as a CD or DVD that is not included in the version you purchased, you may download this material at http://booksupport.wiley.com. For more information about Wiley products, visit www.wiley.com.

Library of Congress Cataloging-in-Publication Data:

Names: Bregman, Peter, author.
Title: Leading with emotional courage : how to have hard conversations,
    create accountability, and inspire action on your most important work /
    Peter Bregman.
Description: Hoboken : Wiley, 2018. | Includes index. |
Identifiers: LCCN 2018008605 (print) | LCCN 2018012980 (ebook) | ISBN
    9781119505679 (epub) | ISBN 9781119505686 (pdf) | ISBN 9781119505693
    (hardback)
Subjects: LCSH: Leadership. | Personnel management. | BISAC: BUSINESS &
    ECONOMICS / Management. | BUSINESS & ECONOMICS / Leadership. | BUSINESS &
    ECONOMICS / Human Resources & Personnel Management.
Classification: LCC HD57.7 (ebook) | LCC HD57.7 .B734 2018 (print) | DDC
    658.4/092—dc23
LC record available at https://lccn.loc.gov/2018008605

Cover Design: Wiley
Cover Illustration: © RedKoalaDesign/iStockphoto

Printed in the United States of America

SKY10032401_010722

To Ann Bradney and Jessica Gelson
You are remarkable women, leaders, teachers
You inspire me to feel everything
The world is a better place because of you
Thank you

CONTENTS

ELEMENT TWO

Chapter 27
Focus Where It Matters   123
Four Areas to Focus Your Attention

Chapter 28
Use Your Focus as a Filter   127
Use Your First Day Back from Vacation to Energize Your Focus

Chapter 29
You Can't Say It Enough   131
The Mouthwash Principle: For Energized Focus, Rinse and Repeat

Chapter 30
And Sometimes It's Better to Say Less   135
If You Want People to Listen, Stop Talking

PART TWO   FOCUS THEIR ENERGY   139

Chapter 31
Gifted, Game, and Generous   141
Three Qualities All Leaders Need to Cultivate Within Their Teams

Chapter 32
Engage from the Beginning   145
The Farm-to-Table Method of Focusing the Energy of Your Team

Chapter 33
Helping Others Be Trustworthy   149
The Secret to Ensuring Follow-Through

ELEMENT FOUR

CULTIVATE EMOTIONAL COURAGE   165

WHY YOU SHOULD READ THIS BOOK

Think of a hard conversation you know you should have with someone that you haven't initiated. Do you have one in mind?

Now, consider why you haven't had the conversation.

Is it because you don't know what you want to say? I'm betting you know exactly what you want to say. Is it because you haven't had the opportunity to say it? I'm guessing you've already missed a few ripe opportunities to raise this uncomfortable issue. Is it because you don't know *how* to say it? I'm sure you're struggling with finding the perfect words. But why do you need perfect words? Adequate words should be enough.

So, why haven't you had the conversation?

Because it's scary.

As you think about it, your heart rate quickens, your adrenaline flows, your sweat rises to the surface. What if they lash back or get defensive or blame you? What if they simply stare at you and go all passive-aggressive? What if they get meaner afterwards? What if they gossip about you to others? Or maybe you're afraid of your own response. What if *you* lose control and fly into a rage and do things you will regret later?

That would be uncomfortable (to say the least). You would have to feel things that you don't want to feel.

And *that*, it turns out, is what holds you back.

What's hard — what actually derails us from acting powerfully in our lives, in our relationships, at work, in the world — is discomfort. The *discomfort* of follow-through.

On the surface, it seems like the key to follow-through is the courage to act. And it is. But what underlies the courage to act?

The courage to feel. Emotional courage. And that is what this book will help you develop.

If You Are Willing to Feel Everything, You Can Do Anything.

Any gap you have in emotional courage limits your freedom to act. When you avoid feeling, it's a huge drain on your productivity and your organizational outcomes.

I know this because my company, Bregman Partners, helps leaders and teams work more effectively together to get massive traction on their most important work. Our focus is on strategy execution — getting difficult things done — and our coaches help people move through the blocks and obstacles that prevent them from contributing their maximum potential.

Over time, we have seen just about every obstacle imaginable — people coming up against silos, politics, culture, clients, the marketplace, and more.

But, far and away the biggest block to contributing their maximum potential is invariably self-imposed — underdeveloped emotional courage — their resistance to following through on uncomfortable actions. If they don't follow through — if they don't have that hard conversation — then they won't have to feel the hard feelings. So they don't follow through.

Take Brad,[1] for example, CEO of a financial services firm. He was managing a difficult turnaround of his sales organization and had decided that he needed to fire his head of sales, who was a nice guy but who wasn't performing. Three months later, he still hadn't fired him. I asked him why. His answer? "I'm a wimp!"

---

[1] Throughout the book, company and individual's names and some details may have been changed.

No, he's not a wimp. He's a normal human being. Like you, like me. And he is stuck. Just as, at times, you and I are.

More than anything, our collective lack of emotional courage – our unwillingness to feel the hard feelings that arise when we follow through on difficult tasks – is what prevents us and our teams from moving forward.

The opposite is also true (and very exciting). If you are willing to feel everything, you can get massive traction on your most important work, and your organization can achieve great things in the world. You can close the gap between strategy and execution.

That is why I wrote this book. And it's why you should read it.

This book will help you grow your emotional courage. And growing your emotional courage is at the root of all your success. It will enable you to have hard conversations, create accountability, and inspire action on your most important work.

That's a bold statement. What makes me think I can make it?

I designed a leadership training to improve people's ability to act – individually and together – by increasing their willingness to feel. Although participants' hopes and goals varied, I'm sure they will feel familiar to you:

"I want to inspire others to follow me."

"I want to communicate with more impact."

"I don't want to shrink from or avoid conflict."

"I want to take more risks."

"I want to follow through on my ideas."

"I don't want to get so defensive when I, or my ideas, are criticized."

"I want more confidence."

"I want to continue to be successful but without all the anxiety."

"I want people to respect me, trust me, follow my lead, and follow through."

"I want our team to work more effectively together."

No matter your age, your role, your position, your title, your profession, your status, your team, don't you want these things too?

Here's how I know that growing your emotional courage is the path:

Eight months after they attended our program, we surveyed participants about the lasting impact. With no interim intervention from us, they experienced increased effectiveness in *all* categories we measured, including:

- Raising hard-to-talk-about issues in a way that initiates important conversations.
- Taking risks that could lead to new possibilities.
- Connecting with people in a way that inspires their commitment.
- Staying grounded in the face of success, failure, or uncertainty.
- Communicating skillfully in the presence of strong emotions.
- Driving the most critical business results.
- Overall leadership effectiveness.

Then they told us that developing their emotional courage had other positive effects on their leadership and their lives:

- Created lasting relationships they could count on.
- Increased their ability to act when they were at their edge.
- Increased their confidence in critical leadership moments.
- Uncovered their unique blind spots and helped them remove those blind spots as obstacles to their success.
- Increased their effectiveness in the face of uncertainty and ambiguity.
- Increased their courage to act.
- Increased their ability to have difficult conversations with productive outcomes.
- Stimulated them to stop procrastinating on important leadership actions.
- Had a positive impact on their career.
- Had a positive impact on their business results.

- Increased their ability to change their behavior.
- Had a lasting impact on their leadership.

You can have these things too. Emotional courage is not a talent that some people are born with and others aren't. It is entirely developable. We all feel things deeply. In fact, that's why we let feelings stop us – we have learned, through experience, that some feelings – shame, embarrassment, rejection, to name a few – are painful. And so we do our best to shut those feelings down, mostly by restricting our behavior so that we don't do things that might invite those feelings. But that strategy is flawed: It makes us much less powerful in the world.

Here's the good news: You had emotional courage when you were younger and you can have it again. It's a coming home, really. And what I have learned from our leadership work is that emotional courage is not just an idea, it's a muscle. And, like all muscles, it grows with exercise. Each time you follow through on a task you might be avoiding, you are working your emotional courage muscle, building it, helping it grow stronger.

Every time you choose to initiate a difficult conversation, you are developing your emotional courage. Every time you take a risk, make a decision, or influence others, you are growing your emotional courage. Even something as seemingly simple as hearing someone's opposing viewpoint or criticism of you without getting defensive – in other words, even listening – that's increasing your emotional courage.

With enough practice, emotional courage will be second nature and, though some things will still feel daunting, many will be less so, and you will have the courage to feel whatever it is you need to feel in order to move ahead.

HOW TO HAVE HARD CONVERSATIONS, CREATE ACCOUNTABILITY, AND INSPIRE ACTION ON YOUR MOST IMPORTANT WORK

To get your most important work done you have to have hard conversations, create accountability, and inspire action. In order to do that, you need to show up powerfully and magnetically in a way that attracts people to trust you and follow you and commit to putting 100% of their effort into a larger purpose, something bigger than all of you. You need to care about others, and connect with them in a way that they feel your care. You need to speak persuasively – in a way that's clear, direct, honest, and reflects your care – while listening with openness, compassion, and love. Even when being challenged. And, of course, you need to follow through – taking brave action to make what's in your head a reality in the world.

In 25 years of working with leaders to do all the above, I have found a pattern, illustrated in Figure I.1. Four essential elements that all great leaders demonstrate. Four ways of showing up that predictably rally people to accomplish what's important to them:

1. You need to be confident in yourself.
2. You need to be connected with others.
3. You need to be committed to a purpose.
4. You need to act with emotional courage.

Most of us are great at only one of the four. Maybe two. But to be a powerful presence – to inspire action – you need to excel at *all four simultaneously.*

If you're confident in yourself, but disconnected from others, everything will be about you and you'll alienate the people around you. If you're connected to others, but lack confidence in yourself, you will betray your own needs and perspectives in order to please

Confident in Yourself

Connected with Others

Committed to Purpose

Emotionally Courageous

Figure I.1   Four essential elements that all great leaders demonstrate.

everyone else. If you're not committed to a purpose, something bigger than yourself and others, you'll lose the respect of those around you as you act aimlessly, failing to make an impact on what matters most. And if you fail to act, powerfully, decisively, and boldly – with emotional courage – your ideas will remain in your head and your goals will remain unfulfilled fantasies.

Consider the following three people who attended our leadership training:

1. Frank, the president of a financial services firm, was thoughtful, aware, and intentional about what he did, why he did it, and how he wanted to impact those around him. He set good boundaries, knew what he needed, and didn't hesitate to speak up for himself. But he wasn't getting the traction he hoped for. The problem was that he often alienated the people around him who, in his view, didn't understand him. When he felt misunderstood, he tried to explain himself, which, to his confusion, annoyed people even more. He knew he wasn't getting the best out of the people around him – they were underperforming – but he wasn't sure what would motivate them or how to do it.

2. Shelly was a well-loved entrepreneur who always took great care of her clients, her employees, and her family. She felt good about her success with other people – she knew how to keep people happy – and they certainly felt great about her. But her company was stalled and she felt exhausted and anxious. Shelly had a sense that something was missing in her life, but wasn't even sure what that meant or what she needed. And she was afraid to make too many changes lest they disrupt the people around her whose needs she prioritized. Shelly was connected to everyone else, and she was willing to give up on herself and even her company – in order to meet their needs.

3. Sanjay was a powerhouse. A turnaround leader. He was the person a company called in when they needed change. He set

high expectations, articulated them clearly, and pursued them with abandon. He was decisive, visionary. He told it like it was. The problem Sanjay faced was that people often failed to deliver to his high expectations. And he just didn't understand why. So he got to the office even earlier, stayed later, created more defined plans, and put more pressure on his employees. None of it helped and he found himself increasingly frustrated and annoyed by their inability to produce. His family complained about how absent he was. His employees complained that he didn't listen to them. Even he felt something was off – he didn't feel good – but he couldn't put his finger on it. So he just focused on the end goal and kept pushing.

Frank, Shelly, and Sanjay each have one element of the four elements. Frank was confident in himself, Shelly was connected to everyone else, and Sanjay was committed to a purpose that was bigger than both himself and others.

And, in key areas, all three of them were missing elements, including the critical fourth element – emotional courage. Frank did not have the courage to be vulnerable to the needs and concerns of others, Shelly was not willing to ask for help, and Sanjay kept himself safe by devoting himself fully to – and hiding behind – his work, avoiding himself and others in the process.

It was costing all of them – personally and professionally. They were frustrated when they could have been joyful, tired when they could have been energized. Their employees were less productive, less inspired, and less collaborative than they could be and than they wanted to be. And the larger purpose of their hard work had stalled.

Maybe you recognize some of these challenges in yourself? Perhaps you are confident and clear but struggle to connect with others? Maybe you give yourself up to please the people around you? Perhaps you throw yourself into work and you neglect yourself and everyone around you? Maybe you hold yourself back in all these areas, hesitant to take risks that might backfire?

That's why emotional courage is so important.

Emotional courage amplifies your power in each of the first three areas. When you are willing to feel, you are willing to act, to take risks. It's a risk to be confident, to believe in yourself. A risk to be open to others. A risk to commit to something bigger than yourself. Confidence, connection, and commitment require that you be communicative, vulnerable, and honest. You will feel exposed. You may be hurt. When you risk your devotion, your reputation, you will face uncertainty, rejection, failure, and insecurity (among other things). You're making a bet – on yourself, on others, on a purpose – and that bet may not play out in your favor. It's a risk. And that's scary.

But if you want to accomplish anything worthwhile, that's a bet you need to make. Those are feelings you'll have to feel.

The skills to have hard conversations, create accountability, and inspire action on your most important work are in this book. Chapter by chapter you will build your confidence, connect with others, deepen your commitment to something bigger than yourself, and hone your emotional courage.

The book is broken into four sections, corresponding to the four elements. Each section has two parts and each part has six short chapters. Part One of each section is about charging and strengthening your power in that particular element and Part Two is about unleashing that power in the world.

Build Your Confidence
- Know Who You Are
- Become Who You Want To Be

Figure I.2 Building confidence creates your foundation.

Element One: Build Your Confidence. You will often hear people say that it's important to be confident, but that's easier said than done. This section will help you *do* it.

- Part One, Know Who You Are, will guide you to find your ground and stand powerfully in who you are.
- Part Two, Become Who You Want to Be, will help you step forward, into the future, to become the person you have the potential to be. (See Figure I.2.)

Connect with Others
- Be Curious and Trusting
- Be Clear and Trustworthy

Figure I.3   Success depends on connecting with others.

Element Two: Connect with Others. Your success in generating alignment and creating collective action is based in your ability to develop relationships with others. This section specifically supports your building deep, trusting relationships you can rely on, and helps you have hard conversations that develop allegiance to you and your larger purpose.

- Part One, Be Curious and Trusting, will guide you to show up with interest and openness to others which, perhaps counterintuitively, is precisely what will create the space for others to be receptive and stay open to you, your thoughts, and your ideas.
- Part Two, Be Clear and Trustworthy, offers very practical direction about what to do and say, and even how to do and say it, so that you come across with clarity and trustworthiness, communicate skillfully even when it's hard, and show up to others in a way that elicits their respect. (See Figure I.3.)

Commit to Purpose

- Energize Your Focus
- Focus Their Energy

Figure I.4   Achieving a common purpose requires focus.

Element Three: Commit to Purpose. Inspiring people to act together requires a shared focus that supersedes any one person's individual interests. This section specifically addresses the challenge of generating accountability and inspiring action toward a common purpose.

- Part One, Energize Your Focus, is about connecting with what you care most about, and establishing a clear, powerful, compelling focus toward a larger purpose.
- Part Two, Focus Their Energy, will help you channel the energy of the key people around you, so that they understand, buy-in, follow-through, and contribute passionately to your larger purpose. (See Figure I.4.)

Cultivate Emotional Courage

- Feel Courageously
- Act Boldly

Figure I.5   Emotional courage feeds – and draws on – confidence, connections, and commitment.

Element Four: Cultivate Emotional Courage. This section is about taking your emotional courage to the next level. Step-by-step you will hone your ability to take risks and follow through on the hard demands of leadership – building your confidence, connecting with others, and committing to a larger purpose.

- Part One, Feel Courageously, will develop your willingness, capacity, and skill to feel everything.
- Part Two, Act Boldly, will develop your risk muscle, by increasing your willingness, capacity, and skill to act, pulling together all four elements of your most powerful self. (See Figure I.5.)

If you read this book cover to cover, it will guide you to methodically grow your capacity to act powerfully in the world. That said, I've designed the book so that you can jump in anywhere. Perhaps you're already confident but need help connecting with others. Or maybe you give up on yourself to please everyone around you. In those cases, you may want to go directly to the parts of the book that most speak to you.

In order to help you do that, I've provided an assessment below that will help you target the areas – and even specific chapters – that may feel most relevant and helpful to you in this moment. The assessment maps directly to the book. Like the book, there are four sections to the assessment and each question relates to a specific chapter. After taking the assessment, you may choose to read a specific section first, or even a specific chapter. Feel free to jump around, or read the book from beginning to end – whatever serves you best.

Assessment Instructions: The following 48 statements correspond directly to the 48 chapters of the book. Each statement reflects the outcome that the designated chapter will help you achieve.

Place a check in the "yes" column if you already consistently live this statement in your life. Place a check in the "No" column if you don't already live this statement, inconsistently live the statement, or if you want to improve in this area. If you are unsure or have any doubt, that's a sign that you should check "No." (To take the assessment online and have your results automatically calculated, go to www .bregmanpartners.com/emotional-courage/resources).

Build Your Confidence
- Know Who You Are
- Become Who You Want To Be

Connect with Others
- Be Curious and Trusting
- Be Clear and Trustworthy

 Commit to Purpose
- Energize Your Focus
- Focus Their Energy

 Cultivate Emotional Courage
- Feel Courageously
- Act Boldly

Figure I.6   Build your confidence.

Element 1: Confidence in Yourself

CH	Part One: Know Who You Are	Yes	No
1	I stay true to myself, even if I know it will disappoint people around me.	☐	☐
2	I remain steady, balanced, and calm no matter what's going on around me.	☐	☐
3	I routinely ask for, and take in, feedback without becoming defensive.	☐	☐
4	I am gentle and compassionate with myself when I struggle or fail.	☐	☐
5	I recognize, and embrace, multiple sides of me, including sides that feel unsavory.	☐	☐
6	I care much more about being useful than about being recognized.	☐	☐

CH	Part Two: Become Who You Want to Be	Yes	No
7	I clearly see the person I want to be and the future I want to create.	☐	☐
8	I clearly see the ways in which I already am the person I want to become.	☐	☐
9	I put aside distractions to focus on the future I want to create.	☐	☐
10	I invest my energy wisely and strategically.	☐	☐
11	I work a balanced amount (I am not a workaholic).	☐	☐
12	I laugh easily and often.	☐	☐

Build Your Confidence
• Know Who You Are
• Become Who You Want To Be

Connect with Others
• Be Curious and Trusting
• Be Clear and Trustworthy

Commit to Purpose
• Energize Your Focus
• Focus Their Energy

Cultivate Emotional Courage
• Feel Courageously
• Act Boldly

Figure I.7   Connect with others.

Element 2: Connect with Others

CH	Part One: Be Curious and Trusting	Yes	No
13	People clearly know and feel that I trust them (even when we disagree).	☐	☐
14	People clearly know and feel that I listen to them (even when we disagree).	☐	☐
15	People clearly know and feel that I am curious about them and don't draw conclusions about them.	☐	☐
16	I approach sticky problems with curiosity and creativity.	☐	☐
17	I make myself useful in whatever way is needed to support what others need.	☐	☐
18	I am well-liked by all (even people who disagree with me).	☐	☐

	Part Two: Be Clear and Trustworthy		
19	I energize the people around me to move forward.	☐	☐
20	I don't procrastinate on the conversations I'm afraid of having.	☐	☐
21	I am skilled at initiating hard conversations.	☐	☐
22	I am skilled at communicating in the midst of heated emotions.	☐	☐
23	I easily admit when I've made a mistake or I'm wrong.	☐	☐
24	People clearly know and feel that I appreciate them (even when we disagree).	☐	☐

Build Your Confidence
• Know Who You Are
• Become Who You Want To Be

Connect with Others
• Be Curious and Trusting
• Be Clear and Trustworthy

Commit to Purpose
• Energize Your Focus
• Focus Their Energy

Cultivate Emotional Courage
• Feel Courageously
• Act Boldly

Figure I.8 Commit to purpose.

Element 3: Commit to Purpose

CH	Part One: Energize Your Focus	Yes	No
25	I give my all to achieve what I'm most passionate about.	☐	☐
26	I am clear about the small number of things that "move the needle" on what matters most.	☐	☐
27	I focus my time and energy on the small number of things that matter most and I let go of the rest.	☐	☐
28	I have a clear and reliable process that keeps me focused on the small number of things that matter most.	☐	☐
29	I am willing to repeat myself until I'm bored in order to reinforce what matters most.	☐	☐
30	I am willing to stay silent about everything else in order to reinforce what matters most.	☐	☐

	Part Two: Focus Their Energy		
31	My team prioritizes our shared interests over their individual interests.	☐	☐
32	I involve people in the earliest, beginning stages of our work.	☐	☐
33	I have a clear and reliable process that ensures people follow through on their commitments.	☐	☐
34	I have a clear and reliable process that holds people accountable.	☐	☐
35	I truly believe that I need help and I ask for it.	☐	☐
36	I am effective at helping others recover and perform after their mistakes, failures, and struggles.	☐	☐

Build Your Confidence
• Know Who You Are
• Become Who You
  Want To Be

Connect with Others
• Be Curious and Trusting
• Be Clear and Trustworthy

Commit to Purpose
• Energize Your Focus
• Focus Their Energy

Cultivate Emotional Courage
• Feel Courageously
• Act Boldly

Figure I.9   Cultivate emotional courage.

Element 4: Emotional Courage

CH	Part One: Feel Courageously	Yes	No
37	At any given moment, I can identify what I am feeling.	☐	☐
38	I can identify where in my body I feel an emotion.	☐	☐
39	I can easily manage the tension of not getting what I want.	☐	☐
40	I routinely step into the unknown.	☐	☐
41	Pain and discomfort do not dissuade me from doing what needs to be done.	☐	☐
42	I regularly feel a wide range of emotions at the same time, some of them contradictory.	☐	☐

	Part Two: Act Boldly		
43	I routinely take calculated and bold risks.	☐	☐
44	I intentionally put myself in uncomfortable situations.	☐	☐
45	I make hard decisions quickly.	☐	☐
46	I skillfully tell people hard truths in a way that they can hear it.	☐	☐
47	I regularly try new ways of acting, even when it doesn't feel authentic.	☐	☐
48	I make the highest impact use of each moment.	☐	☐

The results of this assessment reflect your strengths and weaknesses in the Four Elements. Now that you've taken it, you have a good idea where you have room to grow and what sections or chapters of this book will help you the most.

However you choose to move through this book, you will read stories and have opportunities to practice, reflect, course correct, and practice more as you act and lead courageously. You will follow through on the things you care about most. You will take bold action that moves people and work forward.

You'll be better for it.

Those around you will be better for it.

And the world will be better for it.

LEADING
WITH
EMOTIONAL
COURAGE

ELEMENT ONE

BUILD YOUR CONFIDENCE

↗

Build Your Confidence
- Know Who You Are
- Become Who You Want To Be

Connect with Others
- Be Curious and Trusting
- Be Clear and Trustworthy

Commit to Purpose
- Energize Your Focus
- Focus Their Energy

Cultivate Emotional Courage
- Feel Courageously
- Act Boldly

Just about everything meaningful and worthwhile you choose to do in the world requires that you have a strong and powerful belief in yourself and your ability to make an impact. If you are easily thrown off balance – or off course – you will have a hard time moving forward in the work that is important to you.

Part One of this section, Know Who You Are, will help you find your balance. It will help you build the kind of confidence that enables you to stay true to yourself, even if it means disappointing another. The chapters in this part will help you find your ground, and stand steady, even in the face of uncertainty, criticism, politics, and chaos. They will help you be gentle with, and accepting of, yourself even during your struggles and failures. They will help you accept and appreciate all parts of yourself, even as you become aware of the parts you may not be so crazy about. And they will help you see yourself fully, even when others don't see you the way you want to be seen. That kind of confidence gives you the freedom to be completely, unapologetically yourself.

Part Two of this section, Become Who You Want to Be, helps you build on who you are now to become the person you need to become to achieve what's most important to you. The chapters in this part will help you focus on the future you want to create, recognize and appreciate the things you are already doing to achieve that future, and avoid the distractions that might block your path to getting there. These chapters will help you invest your time wisely and strategically, getting your most important work done without losing yourself in the process.

PART ONE

KNOW WHO YOU ARE

CHAPTER 1

BE YOURSELF

THE HIGH COST OF CONFORMITY, AND HOW TO AVOID IT

I was biking with my friends Eric and Adam, both far more skilled and experienced mountain bikers than I, on terrain that was slightly beyond my own skill. I thought I could do it.

I was wrong.

I suffered a pretty dramatic crash, falling down a ravine, flipping over a few times, and hitting my (helmeted) head on a tree. Eventually, I ended up in the emergency room – but not before riding another hour.

Everything turned out fine, but continuing after my crash was a poor decision. Not only was I riding injured, but, because I was tight with fear, I fell many more times.

Why didn't I stop? I wish I could say it was bravery but, the truth is, it was nothing of the kind. I kept riding, quite simply, because Eric and Adam kept riding.

There are a host of tangled reasons, of course: I didn't want to disrupt their ride or feel like a wimp who couldn't handle a few falls, or give up on something that I started. But the real reason I continued? Because they did.

It turns out that I'm not alone. The research shows that, even as adults, we tend to conform to the behaviors of those around us. If your colleagues take sick days, then you'll start taking them too. If your colleagues are messy, you'll become more messy, too.

5

Which is not such a big deal, really. Until it is.

Take the Volkswagen diesel scandal, for example. Volkswagen installed software in diesel cars to manipulate emissions tests and illegally sidestep pollution standards. They lied to millions of consumers.

When Michael Horn, head of Volkswagen Group of America, testified at a congressional hearing, he said that he believed only "a couple of software engineers" were responsible.

Seriously? Only a couple? At the time of the scandal, Volkswagen employed 583,000 people. Surely more than two people knew about this deception. Why didn't anybody say anything?

One reason might be that aggressive and pressured goal setting can lead to cheating, lying, and misdirected efforts (to avoid punishment of failure). And certainly we've heard that Volkswagen's culture was brutally focused on achieving their goals.

But seven years and 11 million cars later, you would think that *someone* would say *something*. But they didn't. Because saying something, when nobody else is saying anything, is really, really hard.

Still, that's what we must do if we don't want to lose ourselves to conformity. It takes confidence to stand apart. To be willing to move in a different direction than others. But it builds confidence too. Every time we choose to be who we are, different from those around us, we're *developing* our confidence. The real question then – for you and me – is how can we resist the pull of conformity and stand courageously in truth and right? How can we live the values that make us trustworthy? How can we be true to ourselves in the midst of intense pressure to conform?

1. The first step is to have clear, strong, and committed values. What do you believe in? And how resolutely are you willing to stand behind those beliefs? Are you willing to be vulnerable? To be embarrassed? To be disliked? To be fired? Powerful, trustworthy people answer yes to all of those questions.

2. The next step is to want to see what is going on around you. Can you see it for what it is?

3. Finally, you need the courage to act when something is going on that is out of sync with your values. To say something. To stand up to power, if that's what it takes. And to do it skillfully and with respect, so that you are not only more likely to succeed, but also to preserve the relationships around you where possible.

This last one – courage to act – is the most difficult. Difficult because it requires that we go against the norm of what is going on around us. And, while that might be something we're born with, it doesn't come naturally to us as adults. It takes practice.

Practice in small ways. Keep common workspace clean when everyone around you is leaving it messy. Work every day even when the people around you are taking sick days. Act or speak differently than the people around you. Choose not to eat dessert or drink when everyone else is. Make different choices than others.

When you do those things, slow down enough to feel its impact on you. Knowing you can tolerate that feeling is the secret to escaping its hold on you. And that gives you the freedom to act in line with your values.

If we assume that more than a couple of individuals knew about the software scam at Volkswagen, then they fell down in one of these three steps. Either they weren't clear, strong, and committed to the value of truth and honesty in business. Or they chose not to see. Or they lacked the courage to say something.

But I know that it's hard. They would have been risking their friends, their jobs. They would have violated the trust of some coworkers in order to maintain the trust of other coworkers and customers. They would have had to stand alone. Those are hard decisions to make.

I should know. I biked an hour longer than I should have, injured and falling, because I lacked the courage to tell my friends – supportive, caring friends – that I had had enough.

I guess I needed more practice finding my ground ...

CHAPTER 2

FIND YOUR GROUND

STAY STEADY, BALANCED, AND CALM

I was having one of those days — maybe you're familiar with them — when I felt like a passenger on a fast, jerky subway train, holding the handrail tight just to stay standing, each turn throwing me off balance.

I gave a presentation that received a standing ovation and left the stage on top of the world. Then I read an angry email from someone and became angry myself. Following that, I did a fun on-radio interview and I was energized. A little later, I received feedback that I talked too much in a meeting and I was embarrassed and disappointed in myself.

Each new experience sent me flying in a different direction. My concept of myself was simply a reflection of my latest interaction. I was out of control, a victim to the whim of circumstance.

I'm not proud to admit this, but in the past I had a system that helped me remain confident and feeling good in the midst of the turbulence: I took credit for the positive experiences while blaming the negative ones on others. That presentation I did? Yeah, I'm good! The feedback that I talked too much? Clearly that person has her own issues.

The problem with that system, of course, is that it requires a level of denial that anyone with a shred of intellectual honesty and a

9

modicum of self-awareness would find difficult to sustain. Eventually, reality overcomes self-deception.

No, I needed something more solid on which to build my confidence, an alternative to being tossed around by external events that didn't rely on pretense.

Then, one day, sitting in meditation, I found it.

As I followed my breath in and out, I noticed something I hadn't paid much attention to before. And paying attention to it changed everything.

That something I noticed? My self.

By self, I don't mean the person who was breathing, I mean the person who was watching the breathing. This is a little difficult to describe, so bear with me here.

Your self doesn't change when circumstances around you change. You're not a different person after a compliment than you are after an insult. You might feel different things after each, but you aren't, essentially, a different person.

And unless you find solid footing in your consistent, unshakable self, you'll be thrown off balance and lose your way. You'll change your mind at the first resistance. You'll become overconfident when praise abounds. And you'll lose all your confidence in the face of criticism. Then you'll make poor decisions, just to feel better.

Connecting with your self is the key to maintaining your equanimity, your peace, your clarity, and your judgment, even in the face of changing circumstances and pressures.

So how can you find your self?

One of the great gifts of meditation is that it exposes your self. As it turns out, it's surprisingly easy to find because it's always there, watching.

Don't take my word for it, see for yourself. Try it now: Sit comfortably, shut your eyes, and breathe naturally. Follow your breath as it goes in and out of your body without thinking about anything in particular except your breath.

Soon enough, you will notice that your mind is thinking about something. Maybe it's wondering what you're doing or what you look like doing it. Maybe it's trying to solve a problem. Maybe it just remembered something you forgot to do.

The person noticing those thoughts? That's you. That's your self. Your self just noticed "thinking."

See, Descartes was wrong when he said "I think, therefore I am." It's more accurate to say "I watch myself think, therefore I am."

You are not your thinking. You are the person watching your thinking. That little distinction is the difference between feeling your feelings and *being* them—and it's critically important. When you *feel* anger, you're in control of what you do next. When you *are* angry, you've lost control.

The part of you that observes your thoughts and feelings is steady and wise and trustworthy. Identifying with your stable, predictable self builds your confidence because it makes you a stable, predictable person and leader, one who doesn't get tossed around by random events and the decisions of the people around you.

Being connected with your self will give you the confidence to act even in risky situations because you'll know, no matter what happens, that you'll be fine. Even though everything around you may change – how much money you have, whether you have a job, whether you're married, and so on – your self will still be there, observing.

In other words, even in failure, you'll be able to let the part of you that did not change as a result of the failure see what it feels like to fail. Then, when you realize your self is still intact, you'll get up and try again.

The same holds true for your successes. Having a strong relationship with your self will make you incorruptible. Success can still feel good; you just won't define yourself by it. Your confidence won't depend on it.

How can you best cultivate your relationship with your self? The most reliable way I have found is by meditating. Which doesn't always have to mean sitting on a cushion on the floor. A few settling breaths to engage the observer in you are all it takes. The more you practice, the better you get.

Yesterday I was, literally, on one of those twisty-turny subway rides and I decided to play a game I used to play as a teenager. I got into a stable stance and let go of the handrails. Subway surfing.

As the train lurched, I absorbed the changes by shifting my weight and keeping my balance, staying upright and steady, and noticing what this particular kind of fun feels like.

Being who you are enables you to stay steady in the midst of external influences – success and failure, or praise and criticism. Staying curious about how you're perceived, and learning from those perceptions – without losing your self – will deepen your understanding of, and ultimately your confidence in, yourself …

CHAPTER 3

STAY CURIOUS ABOUT YOURSELF

HOW TO ASK FOR FEEDBACK
THAT WILL ACTUALLY HELP YOU

"So," I asked Mary, "Do you have any feedback for me? What can I do better next time?"

We had just finished delivering a leadership training to senior executives at a large financial services company. My working relationship with Mary was a little tricky; she was my co-trainer and also my client, since she worked full time at the bank.

Mary did have some feedback for me, which was insightful and useful. After I thanked her, she asked me if I had any feedback for her.

I did. There were three things I thought she could do that would make her a more powerful, effective trainer. But I never got them out. As soon as I began to point out the first one, she interrupted me.

"You don't understand," she told me, and then explained all the reasons why she had acted the way she did. She was polite, but defensive. If she were my employee, or if I were coaching her, I would have pushed through her defensiveness. Maybe I should have anyway. But I made a quick judgment call that it wasn't in my interests and wouldn't, ultimately, help our working relationship. So I stopped.

Receiving feedback is hard. It can be difficult to draw out the truth from the people around you – people who may be too nice to share the full picture or too intimidated to be honest.

And yet it's a gift to know what people are really thinking about you. This is true in all realms of your life – knowing how your partner or spouse feels can mean the difference between a connected relationship and a dysfunctional one.

Getting useful feedback can be the fastest route to understanding yourself fully; it's the best way (perhaps the only way) to uncover your blind spots. While it's not always an accurate reflection of who you are – it often isn't – it's always an accurate reflection of how you're perceived. And knowing how you're perceived is critically important if you want to increase your influence and inspire action on what's most important to you.

There's a confidence-building upside, too. Confidence works in a constructive cycle – the more you do things that require confidence, the more confident you become. Yes, it takes confidence to hear other people's perspectives about you. Meanwhile, receiving their opinions without shrinking builds your confidence.

Being good at receiving feedback – at staying curious about *yourself* – is especially important at work, because your colleagues are less likely to push past your defensiveness and more willing to write you off if they have a hard time working with you. If that happens, you'll never know why – since you won't have heard the feedback – so you'll keep repeating the same mistakes.

Here's how to increase your chances of hearing the truth:

1. **Be clear that you want honest feedback.** Let people know they're doing you a favor by being truthful. "Don't be nice," you can tell them. "Be helpful." Explain that you want to get the most out of the conversation, and it won't work if they hold back.

2. **Focus on the future.** Ask what you can do better going forward as opposed to what you did wrong in the past. When you ask people what you can do to be more effective in the future, they tend to be more honest.

3. **Probe more deeply.** Don't just ask once. Give people multiple opportunities to give you real feedback, to increase the chances they'll feel comfortable doing so. It can be helpful to ask about specific situations – for example, what could you do better in a particular future meeting?

4. **Listen without judgment.** Don't judge any feedback you receive, whether it's positive or negative. Thank people for being honest with you and let them know that you find their observations and opinions helpful. If they think that you really want the truth and you won't react poorly to negative feedback, they'll be more willing to be completely honest. If you get defensive about anything, they'll stop and be polite.

5. **Write down what they say.** This tactic accomplishes two things. A little silence communicates that you're taking feedback seriously and it gives those offering it time to think about what else they might say. Often they'll volunteer a second – and very important – thought while waiting for you to finish writing.

Not long after our awkward attempt to trade feedback, Mary left the financial services firm and joined a different company, which she left after a short time.

It may be hard to hear the truth, but, in the long run, it's even harder not to.

Which doesn't mean that it will feel pleasant. It often won't, which is why self-compassion is such an important tool as you build your confidence and stand steady in who you are ...

CHAPTER 4

ACCESS SELF-COMPASSION

THE PROBLEM WITH HIGH EXPECTATIONS

At 5 a.m. I was lying in bed, awake, thinking. Actually, thinking is too generous a word for what I was doing. I was perseverating.

I was about to buy a new bicycle, and I couldn't decide on the color. I tried to visualize the bike and imagine how I would feel riding it in each color. I weighed the options, hoping one would rise as the right choice.

I'd already gone online numerous times to look at the bike, even interrupting important work to do so, and I'd gone back to the bike store twice. I'd asked countless people which color they thought I should get, pulling out my iPhone to show them the options.

I'm embarrassed about this. I'm supposed to be efficient and productive. I'm supposed to be confident. But there I was, wasting time, asking other people to help me choose my favorite color. This is not who I want to be.

But, clearly, it is who I am. Much as I'd like to deny it, I can be indecisive and insecure.

That's hard for me to admit, so I tried to avoid facing it.

I blamed others: Maybe it was my parents' fault – they made so many decisions for me that I never learned to have confidence in my own choices. Or maybe it was the bike company's fault for offering

17

so many colors – there's compelling research proving that the more alternatives we have, the harder it is to choose.

I minimized my struggle: I make lots of important decisions, so who cares if I can't make the insignificant ones?

And I tried to follow a process: First eliminate the obvious no's, then if it's still unclear, they all must be fine and I'll just choose any one of the remaining colors.

None of this worked. A week later, I had still not decided.

One night as I lay awake feeling the shame of my ineptitude, I began to think about my daughter. She used to have difficulty controlling her impulses and she fell quickly into conflicts with friends. How often have I scolded her or given her unsolicited pushy advice, annoyed that she acted the way she did?

I'd assumed that, if she had to, she would change. But, from the vantage of my own struggle, I realized how wrong I'd been. My daughter was doing the absolute best she could. And my judgment of her behavior – of her – only made her feel and behave worse.

That's when it really hit me: My expectations of everyone, including myself, are counterproductively high.

High expectations can have a positive effect; people need a high bar to stretch toward. But I think many of us take it too far. We slip so easily into criticisms of ourselves and those around us – family, friends, coworkers, public figures – that we no longer expect people to be human beings. And when we shame ourselves and others for failing, we make things worse. We contribute to pain while nurturing impotence.

When we face weakness – ours or someone else's – it doesn't help to blame someone or something, pretend it's not important, or simply decide to change. And it's not sufficient to identify a three-step process to fix the problem. So what does help?

Here's the best I've come up with: compassion.

As far as I can tell, for advice to be useful at all, it needs to be preceded by compassion. Yes my daughter needed support, guidance, instruction, and advice. But she needed compassion first. As the saying goes: Be kind, for everyone you meet is fighting a hard battle. That certainly includes me. And, I'm betting, you. Being compassionate will probably make us better, more effective people. If not, at least it will reduce the suffering that accompanies weakness. And it will most certainly make us nicer to each other and to ourselves.

Compassion is also a critical foundation for your self-confidence. If we are kind to ourselves, we will feel good about ourselves and we will believe in ourselves more. But it's not just about self-compassion; We often project our foibles onto other people – so compassion for them is really compassion for ourselves, and a critical building block of self-confidence (more on that in the next chapter).

Eventually, I bought a bike. I rode it home. Then, the next day, I woke up at five in the morning again, second-guessing my decision, thinking I should have bought a different color. I berated myself momentarily and then I remembered: This is who I am. It's not perfect. But it's the best I can do. And that, I trust, is good enough.

And good enough is better than perfect because it allows us to acknowledge – and be okay with – all of who we are. We can't confidently know who we are while repressing some part of who we are (confidence that depends on repression is fragile). And repression doesn't make things go away, it just leads us to push those things into the shadows, and project them onto other people. At which point, most likely, we'll be controlled by – and even become – the very things we hate. But there's a way to avoid that – by learning more about ourselves, and building our confidence, all at the same time ...

CHAPTER 5

EMBRACE YOUR SHADOW

HOW TO AVOID BECOMING THE PERSON YOU HATE

I was so angry my whole body was shaking. I stared at Günther with hate, my left hand in a fist and my right hand gripping a tennis racket as a weapon. I was ready to kill him.

Was this really me?

I was in an intense workshop – The Radically Alive Leader – led by Ann Bradney. There were 23 of us from around the world – many from countries experiencing tremendous violence – and the topic had turned to war.

One by one people stood up – people from the United States, Colombia, Somalia, Mexico, Israel – and spoke about the cruelty they had experienced in their countries. As I heard about family members being kidnapped, raped, or killed, people being bombed and forced to live in refugee camps, my empathy for the victims and my anger at the perpetrators intensified.

Then a quiet woman named Nancy spoke. "We all participate in one way or the other," she said, "We are all guilty."

I could no longer restrain myself. "We're all guilty?" I burst at Nancy. "Really? How about the babies who are dying or the women who have been raped? Are they guilty too? Guilty just like the rapists? That's ridiculous!"

21

The room went silent.

Nancy shrank, and I didn't care. Actually, that's not true – I did care. I loved it. It felt great to lash out. I felt powerful. I felt safe from the violence, righteous. And I felt relieved, as the tension that was building inside me began to subside.

Then Ian, who hadn't yet said a word, spoke into the silence. He asked me if I could see myself killing, if I were in, say, Somalia. I was quick to respond "no."

"You scare me," Ian said.

I scared him? I was the one showing outrage at evil! He shouldn't be scared of me; He should be scared of people who *could* see themselves killing.

But Ian was on to something deep and important. Something we all need to understand: When empathy plays favorites, we should all be scared.

It makes us feel better to separate ourselves from people whose behavior we don't like. It makes us feel moral, safe, and beyond reproach. But it's a false confidence. Separating the other people as evil means we are more likely to lash out at them and, before we know it, become cruel ourselves.

I am not saying that we should excuse violence or poor behavior. There must be consequences to people who act destructively. But psychologically separating ourselves from them makes us dangerous.

It didn't take long for me to learn that lesson firsthand.

I was still filled with emotion from the last conversation when Günther, a German man, started yelling in German, and slamming a tennis racket onto a large foam block, one of the tools that Ann uses in her workshop to get energy moving.

Every time the racket slammed down, I flinched. His accent, the yelling, and the slamming brought me back to my family's memories of the Holocaust. My mother and her family were in hiding in France during the war, and her newborn sister, Ariel, was killed by a doctor who gave her milk that was too thick. He said he did it because she was Jewish.

I imagined Günther in a Nazi uniform, cold eyes peering out behind a low-hanging army cap, emblazoned with a swastika. I was flooded with rage, sadness, and fear. My whole body was shaking. I pictured baby Ariel, dead, wrapped in a blanket, as I picked up the racket.

I slammed the racket on the cube with all my strength. "Stop it," I screamed, completely swept up in the moment. "Stop screaming. Stop the hatred. Stop the violence."

In that moment, I could have killed Günther.

But Günther isn't a Nazi. He's a software developer with a German accent.

In other words, I didn't want to kill Günther for something he had done. I wanted to kill him for something he represented. For his accent.

In that moment – and I feel chills down my spine as I write this – Günther wasn't the Nazi. I was.

In different circumstances – perhaps raised by a parent who taught us differently – who's to say what choices we might make? Any one of us is capable of just about anything. And unless we acknowledge that, we are at greater risk of becoming the person we fear the most. We're more likely to lash out against others to defend our view of ourselves.

This is not just about world leadership and violence; it's about mundane living and everyday relationships, as well. Any time we think or say, in disbelief, "Can you believe what that person did? What kind of person does that? I just can't understand her!" we are separating ourselves from other people, making them essentially bad and us essentially good.

When we do that, we are, at worst, dangerous, and, at best, weak leaders. And our underlying confidence in ourselves decreases because it's built on a house of cards. On how we want see ourselves vs. who we are.

Holding the racket, angry enough to want to kill – was that really me? Yes. At times it may be you, too. Though disturbing, this is a good thing to admit. It's only when we have enough confidence to feel the racket in our own hands – to look at that dark part of ourselves with our eyes open – that we can fully know ourselves. And that is when we are trustworthy to act powerfully.

The picture I'm painting of myself – of you – is complex. We are many things, often contradictory. Since the secrets we hide about ourselves make us insecure and vulnerable to being "found out," acknowledging all parts of ourselves, including our shadows, allows us to stand strongly and confidently with nothing to lose and nothing to prove. From that place, we can stop running ourselves ragged trying to "be" someone, trying to matter to everyone else, and start to live the life that matters *to us* ...

CHAPTER 6

IT'S NOT ALL ABOUT ACHIEVEMENT

STOP WORRYING ABOUT HOW MUCH YOU MATTER

For many years – almost as long as he could remember – Shane owned and ran a successful pub in his small town in Ireland. Shane was well known around town. He had lots of friends, many of whom he saw when they came to eat and drink, and he was happy.

Eventually, Shane decided to sell his establishment. Between his savings and the sale, he made enough money to continue to live comfortably. He was ready to relax and enjoy all his hard work.

Except that almost immediately, he became depressed. That was 15 years ago and not much has changed.

I've seen a version of Shane's story many times. The CEO of an investment bank. A famous French singer. The founder and president of a grocery store chain. A high-level government official. And these are not just stories – they're people I know (or knew) well.

They have several things in common: They were busy and highly successful. They had enough money to live more than comfortably for as long as they lived. And they all became seriously depressed as they got older.

What's going on?

The typical answer is that people need purpose in life and when we stop working, we lose purpose. But many of the people I see in this situation continue to work. The French singer continued to sing. The investment banker ran a fund.

Perhaps getting older is simply depressing. But we all know people who continue to be happy well into their late nineties. And some of the people who fall into this predicament are not particularly old.

I think the problem is much simpler, and the solution is more reasonable than working or staying young forever.

People who achieve financial and positional success are masters at doing things that make and keep them relevant. Their decisions affect many others. Their advice lands on eager ears.

In many cases, if not most, they derive their self-concept, self-confidence, and a strong dose of self-worth from the fact that what they do and what they say – in many cases even what they think and feel – matters to others.

Think about Shane. If he changed his menu or his hours of operation, or hired someone new, it directly affected the lives of the people in his town. Even his friendships were built, in large part, on who he was as a pub owner. What he did made him relevant in the community.

Relevancy, as long as we maintain it, is rewarding on almost every level. But when we lose it? Withdrawal can be painful.

True confidence comes from mastering the exact opposite of what we've spent a lifetime pursuing. We need to master irrelevancy.

This is not only a retirement issue. Many of us are unhealthily – and ultimately unhappily – tied to mattering. It's leaving us overwhelmed and overbusy, responding to every request, ring, and ping with the urgency of a fireman responding to a six-alarm fire. For many of us, our self-confidence is dependent on being that necessary.

How we adjust – both within our careers and after them – to not being that important may matter more than mattering.

If we lose our jobs, adjusting to irrelevancy without falling into depression is a critical survival skill until we land another job. If managers and leaders want to grow their teams and businesses, they need to allow themselves to matter less so others can matter more and become leaders themselves. At a certain point in our lives, and at certain times, we matter less. The question is: Can you be okay with that?

How does it feel to just sit with others? Can you listen to someone's problem without trying to solve it? Can you happily connect with others when there is no particular purpose to that connection?

Many of us (though not all) can happily spend a few days by ourselves, knowing that what we're doing doesn't matter to the world. But a year? A decade?

Still, there is a silver lining to this kind of irrelevancy: freedom.

When your purpose shifts like this, you can do what you want. You can take risks. You can be courageous. You can share ideas that may be unpopular. You can live in a way that feels true and authentic. In other words, when you stop worrying about the impact of what you do, you can be a fuller version of who you are.

Irrelevancy doesn't have to hurt your confidence – it can build it. It gives you the space to find fulfillment in yourself as opposed to the external reinforcements you obviously can't rely on.

So what does being comfortable with the feeling of irrelevancy – even the kind of deep irrelevancy involved in ending a career – really look like? It may be as straightforward as doing things simply for the experience of doing them. Taking pleasure in the activity versus the outcome, your existence versus your impact.

Here are some small ways you might start practicing irrelevancy right away:

- Check your e-mail only at your desk and only a few times a day. Resist the temptation to check your e-mail first thing in the morning or at every brief pause.
- When you meet new people, avoid telling them what you do. During the conversation, notice how frequently you are driven to make yourself sound relevant (sharing what you did the other day, where you're going, how busy you are). Notice the difference between speaking to connect and speaking to make yourself look and feel important.

- When someone shares a problem, listen without offering a solution (if you do this with employees, an added advantage is that they'll become more competent and self-sufficient).
- Try sitting on a park bench without doing anything, even for just a minute (then try it for five or 10 minutes).
- Talk to a stranger (I did this with my cab driver this morning) with no goal or purpose in mind. Enjoy the interaction – and the person – for the pleasure of it.
- Create something beautiful and enjoy it without showing it to anyone. Take note of beauty that you have done nothing to create.

Notice what happens when you pay attention to the present without needing to fix or prove anything. When you allow yourself to simply be yourself. Notice how, even when you're irrelevant to the decisions, actions, and outcomes of the world around you, you can feel the pleasure of simple moments and purposeless interactions.

Notice how, even when you feel irrelevant, you can matter to yourself. And then notice how, when you matter to yourself, your confidence grows.

Part Two

Become Who You Want to Be

CHAPTER 7

FIND CLARITY

WHAT'S YOUR ONE BIG THEME?

At least once a year, I think about my past year and plan for my next. What do I want to repeat? What do I want to do differently?

I usually start with everything I want to do differently. And the list is long.

I eat way too much – well past my point of being full – and leave almost every meal uncomfortable. I feel scattered in my day, focusing on too many things at once, switching rapidly from one thing to the next. I react to what's in front of me too often rather than making strategic choices about where to spend my time. I treat many of my relationships more as transactions than deep connections, appreciating people for what they do for me rather than who they are. In fact, I treat myself that way too, valuing myself for my performance more than my existence. My writing has felt more rushed lately as I produce more and enjoy less. I won't bore you with the rest, but I assure you there's more.

Normally, I would do what we usually do in the business world: Develop a long list of things to do to correct these problems, a series of development plans to improve my performance in each area. I'd learn about new diets, tell myself to stop multitasking, create a plan for improving each one of my relationships, cordon off more time for writing, and so on.

But here's the problem with development plans: They're over-whelming and disconnected. By the end, I'd have 10 different plans for 10 different things I want to change, and I'd make little headway in each. It's just too much – too hard to act on and too easy to abandon. It doesn't build my success; it frustrates it. It doesn't build my confidence; it erodes it.

As I looked at my list this year, I decided to approach it differently.

First, I took a deep breath and realized that I was neglecting what went well.

This year was not easy but, thank God, it's been good. I recently collected feedback from my CEO clients and it's clear that they feel the value I add is more than worth the fees they pay. My books have been selling well. My health seems good, and I'm loving the time I spend with Eleanor and our kids and, just as importantly, they seem to be loving the time they're spending with me. As I appreciated how fortunate I am, I relaxed.

Then, fueled by a feeling of accomplishment, I looked at my list of things to change from a broader perspective, asking myself: What's this really about?

That's when I noticed the theme: I'm moving too fast, trying to do too much.

I realized that pursuing an individual development plan for each thing I wanted to fix would only worsen the problem. I needed to reduce the complexity, not add to it.

So I came up with a single idea – a theme for the coming year – that would positively impact everything I wanted to change.

My theme? Slow down.

My thought was that if I focused only on that, everything else would improve.

And, so far, it has. When I started eating more slowly, my meals effortlessly shifted from three courses to one, and I'm enjoying the food more. Once I slowed down in my conversations, I found myself listen-ing more, talking less, caring more deeply, and enjoying each person more fully.

And what I thought would be a downside has actually been a positive: Slowing down has meant that I can't get as much done, which has forced me to make strategic choices about what to spend my time on and what to ignore. I'm more thoughtful, less scattered, and enjoying my work more fully. Counterintuitively, I'm more productive. And that builds my confidence.

What's nice about a single theme is that it's easy to implement, simple to remember, achievable, and sustainable. It's just one thing.

So what's your one thing? After thinking about the best of who you are and what you've done, list the things you want to change. Then, stare at the list until it reveals the one thing that would impact it the most. Maybe, for you, it's being more aggressive. Or less. Maybe it's slowing down or speeding up or speaking out or being more gentle with yourself and others. If you're not sure, try something for a few weeks and see what changes.

Then, each morning and at various moments throughout the day, remind yourself of your one thing. You won't need to make it your screen saver or write it on a Post-it and place it on your mirror at home. You can if you want, but it's only one thing. It will quickly become second nature as your results reinforce your commitment.

Once you're clear on your one big theme, you'll need to make decisions that give you traction on it. That's how you actualize your commitment to becoming who you most want to be. Where should you start? How about from the solid ground of how amazing you already are …

CHAPTER 8

BECOME MORE OF WHO YOU ARE

YOU'RE ALREADY PRETTY AMAZING

I was opening the mail (the real mail, the one delivered by an actual, live person) and between the bills and solicitations, was a single letter, addressed to me, in sloppy – but recognizable – handwriting.

Recognizable because the handwriting was mine.

At first, I didn't recall sending myself any mail. I opened the letter and began to read. And then I remembered. This was a letter from past Peter to future Peter. At the intensive leadership program I run, participants write a letter to themselves that we send to them months later. This time, I had written one to myself.

My letter included reflection, assessment, and new commitments. What am I grateful for? Where can I improve?

As I read through it, I couldn't help but laugh. It all sounded so familiar. Not just because I had written it, but because I had written it so many times before. I found my file of previous letters, some years apart, and read through them. They were all, essentially, the same.

For the things I am grateful for, that's fine, but what about my new commitments? How could I get more real traction on them?

As I reflected on this question, and sat with all my letters, I began to see something that had eluded me before, a relationship between what

I'm grateful for and what I want to change that represented a way out of my disheartening cycle of struggling self-improvement.

When I ask myself, "where can I improve?" my list usually comes from my shortcomings, things I don't like about myself. For example, I can talk too much, waste time, move too fast, and focus on low priority things.

So, when I think about what I can improve, I just reverse that list: I should talk less, be more productive, move slower, focus on high priority things.

Trying to fix my shortcomings is familiar. And, with concerted effort, it usually works … for a day or two. But, very quickly, I revert to old behaviors. We just talked about this challenge in the previous chapter. We almost always revert to old behaviors.

Which got me thinking. What if reverting to old behaviors is the goal? I know I can achieve that – it's what I do anyway. So what's the process?

1. First, you need to know what you're going for, who you want to become. For me, it's what we talked about in the last chapter, my one theme: Slowing down.

2. Then, the key is to be deliberate about which old behaviors to revert to. That's where the question, "What am I grateful for?" comes in. The things I am grateful for are, by definition, already a part of my life. I am grateful for the undistracted time I spend with my family. For the sense of presence and focus I feel when I am writing. For the times when I really sink in to listen to another, without any need to fix them or the situation they're in. For the clarity I have come to in the past year about what's important to me and to my business – and the time I spend in those areas of focus.

In other words, those things I want to improve on? I'm already doing them. Those are, actually, old behaviors. Habits, even.

When I really sink in to listen to another, without any need to fix them or the situation they're in, I am talking less. When I am present and focused while writing, I am moving more slowly, more deliberately. When I experience undistracted time with my family, I don't feel like I am wasting a minute. When I spend time on my areas of focus, I am settling into my highest priority items.

In this context, the path to improvement may not be effortless, but it should be familiar. And just knowing that can make a difference. It's confidence building.

Consider your one theme and the ways in which you want to improve in order to make it a reality. I am willing to bet that, at least in some areas, the things for which you are grateful mirror the things you want to improve.

Which means that your path to improvement is hidden in your pleasure, not your discontent.

You are most probably already living your life in a way that you aspire to. Perhaps not all the time, but some of the time. You are not moving from nothing to something, you are moving from something to something more. The improvement gap is about consistency more than anything else.

Who are you in those moments when you are grateful? How do you show up? What are you doing? How are you behaving with yourself and others? Go back to those moments of gratitude and bring them into your present.

Reminding yourself of what you have already done in the past is a much more reliable way of shifting your behavior – much more believable, reasonable, doable, repeatable, sustainable – than starting a whole new behavior in the future.

You're remembering, not inventing. You are already the person you aspire to be. Now, with a little focus, you can build on that ...

CHAPTER 9

STAY FOCUSED

YOU NEED TO PRACTICE BEING YOUR FUTURE SELF

I was coaching Sanjay, a leader in a technology firm who felt stuck and frustrated. He wasn't where he wanted to be at this point in his career.

He had come to our coaching session, as usual, prepared to discuss the challenges he was currently facing. This time, it was his plan for conducting compensation conversations with each of his employees. After a few minutes of listening to him talk through his plans, I interrupted him.

"Sanjay, you've had these kinds of conversations before, right?" I asked.

"Yes," he said.

"And, for the most part, you know how to do them, right?"

"Yes," he said again.

"Great. Let's talk about something else."

"But this is what's on my mind right now," he protested. "It's helpful to think it through with you."

"I'm glad it's helpful, Sanjay," I said. "But you don't want me to be merely helpful. You want me to be transformational. And focusing on what's top of mind for you right now is not going to get us there."

You see, the reason Sanjay is stuck – and the reason many of us feel that way – is that we focus on what's present for us at any particular moment.

On the other hand, what most of us want most is to move forward, to become who we want to be, to make our one big theme a reality – and, by definition, paying attention to the present keeps us where we are. So, sure, I can help Sanjay be a better "present" Sanjay. But I will have a much greater impact if I help him become a successful "future" Sanjay.

It's a familiar story: You're busy all day, working nonstop, multitasking in a misguided attempt to knock a few extra things off your to-do list, and as the day comes to a close, you still haven't gotten your most important work done.

Being busy is not the same as being productive. It's the difference between running on a treadmill and running to a destination. They're both running, but being busy is running in place.

If you want to be productive, the first question you need to ask yourself is: Who do I want to be? Another question is: Where do I want to go? Chances are that the answers to these questions represent growth in some direction. And while you can't spend all your time pursuing those objectives, you definitely won't get there if you don't spend any of your time pursuing them.

If you want to be a writer, you have to spend time writing. If you want to be a sales manager, you can't just sell – you have to develop your management skill. If you want to start a new company, or launch a new product, or lead a new group, you have to spend time planning and building your skills and experience.

Here's the key: You need to spend time on the future even when there are more important things to do in the present and even when there is no immediately apparent return to your efforts. In other words – and this is the hard part – if you want to be productive, you need to spend time doing things that feel ridiculously unproductive.

I want to expand my writing abilities, so I have started waking up at 5:30 in the morning to write fiction. Unfortunately – and I am not being humble here – I am a terrible fiction writer. So my writing time feels painfully unproductive. I can't sell it. I can't use it. I can't share it. Honestly, I can hardly bear to read it out loud. I have such a long list of things that actually need to get done, it is almost impossible to justify losing sleep in order to do something so unrelated to my present challenges. I know this is how my clients feel when I ask them to put aside their immediate concerns and focus on more distant challenges.

A question I hear a lot is: What about all the things I actually need to get done? Don't I need to get through my cluttered e-mail box, my pressing conversations, my project plans in order to create space to focus on my future self?

Nope.

That's a trick your busy self plays on you to keep you away from the scary stuff you're not yet good at and that isn't yet productive. Sometimes you need to be irresponsible with your current challenges in order to make real progress on your future self. You have to let the present just sit there, untended. It's not going away and will never end. That's the nature of the present.

You may not end up with an empty email inbox. You may not have the perfect compensation conversations. You may not please everyone. But, as your coach, I'm willing to bet that you will do those things well enough.

It's the other stuff I worry about. The wildly important stuff that never gets done because there's not time or it's not urgent or it's too hard or risky or terrifying. That's the stuff I want to help you work on. That's what leads you to become who you want to be.

Even though Sanjay is delighted at the idea of focusing on his future self, he resists it because it doesn't feel as good as solving his current challenges. He isn't as skilled at it yet. That's why it's his future.

And that is exactly why he needs to focus on it. To do that, he (and you) will have to invest your energy wisely …

CHAPTER 10

BE STRATEGIC AND INTENTIONAL

FIVE STEPS TO INVESTING YOUR ENERGY MORE WISELY

It was a heated political conversation. Honestly, I can't remember about what. What I do remember is that it was heated, frustrating, and tiring.

A few hours later I was still thinking about it and still annoyed. On the one hand, I didn't like the other person's view, or even her mindset. On the other hand, I didn't like my response and how I argued with her. As I continued to turn the conversation over in my mind, a single thought kept popping up:

This is not worth the energy I'm spending on it.

Which matters because I don't have the energy to spare. And, chances are, you don't either. In a recent conversation I had with Tom Rath, author of *Are You Fully Charged?*, he told me that he has asked more than 10,000 people, "Did you have a great deal of physical energy yesterday?" and just 11% said they did.

Which means that 89% of us are operating without much to spare.

There are two sides to this equation: We can fill our energy tanks more fully and frequently, or we can spend our energy more strategically. One or both of these is crucial if we want to bring our strongest, most productive energy to our most important work and life experiences, to becoming who we most want to be.

43

A lot has been written about how to fill our energy tanks more fully. My energy increases when I sleep eight hours, eat healthy foods, stop eating before I'm full, and exercise every day. I also know that having loving relationships, connecting to something bigger than myself, and being emotionally and intellectually engaged all increase my energy.

In other words, I know how to fill my tank. I bet you know how to fill yours too. (If you need ideas, Tom's book offers great ones.)

The question, then, is how strategically are you using the energy you have?

The answer for me: Not very.

When I'm in a conversation, I almost always share my thoughts. In fact, if I am near a conversation, I often share my thoughts. I do far too much work that others in my organization can (and should) do. I involve myself in decisions that others could make just as well or better. And when I am making decisions, I often delay them, struggling to make them perfect even when there are no right answers. Oh, and I check my e-mail constantly.

Those are just the tip of the iceberg of my visible energy spending patterns. There's a whole category of invisible ones that sap my energy even more, such as holding on to frustrations and hurts well past their due date and worrying about the outcome of things over which I have no control.

Once I started to pay attention, I began to see how carelessly – how indiscriminately – I spend my energy. It's a drag on me, on my confidence, and on my future self.

This is worth thinking about because spending our energy wisely is the source of our current productivity, happiness, and confidence. It's the key to becoming who you want to be.

When I invest my energy wisely, I spend it writing, listening, strategizing, teaching, thinking, planning, offering my opinion selectively and with an outcome in mind, and making decisions swiftly (following the advice of the Jewish medieval sage Maimonides: "The risk of a wrong decision is preferable to the terror of indecision.").

It is not simply about productivity. I happily invest my energy in ways that simply bring me joy: My children, reading, interesting conversations with friends, and learning new things for fun, to name a few. These things are a big part of who I am and will continue to be a big part of life for me as I move into my future.

The important thing is to be strategic and intentional about where we put our energy so that we apply it to what matters most to us and become the person we most want to be. Here's how:

1. **Notice your energy.** Where do you spend it? I set my phone to beep at random times during the day as a prompt to notice how I'm spending my energy at that moment – both visibly (doing) and invisibly (thinking). When you look at life with an energy lens, you begin to see things differently. Simply doing this little energy check-in began to change my habits.

2. **Know what matters to you.** Knowing what brings value to your life – joy and productivity – is essential to making smart decisions about where to spend your energy. You might have been in the political argument I mentioned at the beginning of this article and felt blissful. If so, that could be a great use of your energy. For me, it was energy misspent.

3. **Plan wise energy investment.** Once you know which things matter most to you, schedule as many of them into your life as possible. Literally put them in your calendar. Let them crowd out activities that represent energy leaks. This idea of "crowding out" works for thinking, too. Where do you want to spend your mental energy? I find that perseverating over things (or people) that annoy me is almost never a useful way to spend energy. But thinking about what I can learn from something almost always is. Let your learning mind "crowd out" your complaining mind. Scheduling time at the end of the day to glean insights can be incredibly valuable.

4. **Most importantly, plan where not to invest.** Once you begin to notice your energy, you will clearly see things you

do – and ways you think – that are pointless energy drains. Although it's surprisingly hard to stop doing something mid-stream, it's much less painful not to start in the first place. Think of how much easier it is *not* to turn on the television than to stop watching in the middle of a show. Don't enter a conversation that you know will rile you up and get you nowhere.

5. **Finally, don't spend much time thinking about this.** You don't have to get it right, just better than yesterday. And optimizing your energy expenditure can be its own coun-terproductive energy drain. Simply pull yourself out of one useless conversation, stop yourself from responding to one silly email, let go of one nagging thought, and you'll be a more intelligent investor of your energy.

That last point is important. Part of the joy – and the confidence building element – of becoming yourself, is not to try too hard, because it's possible to lose yourself in pursuit of becoming yourself. Here's how to stop that from happening ...

CHAPTER 11

DON'T LOSE YOURSELF IN PURSUIT OF BECOMING YOURSELF

TAKE YOUR LIFE BACK

The waiter was halfway through taking my family's order when his manager called him away.

"Where did the waiter go?" Sophia, our then-seven-year-old, asked.

My son Daniel, five years old at the time, looked at me and then answered, "I think he had to take a conference call."

Even before hearing Daniel's analysis of the waiter's momentary inattention, I knew I had a problem: I work all the time.

I moved from an outside office to a home office because I wanted to spend more time with my family. But now I'm always in my home office. I briefly emerge for moments like dinner and telling bedtime stories, but quickly return "just to finish up a couple of things." I love my work, but it's out of hand.

I desperately need to relax, read fiction, and hang out with people I enjoy. Real confidence comes, in part, from being a balanced human being. But the undertow draws me back to my ocean of tasks, with promises of crossing things off lists and falsely bolstering my self-worth, my self-confidence, with proof of productivity.

Unfortunately our psychological weaknesses are fed by our unmitigated access to the work stream. It's an old story now: We thought our technologies – laptops, smartphones, e-mail – would free us from being stuck to the office but it's backfired: The office is now stuck to us.

We have lost our boundaries. Space used to be a natural demarcation: When you left your office you left your work. But our workspaces have lost their walls.

We need new walls.

Fast forward to Friday night. The table is set beautifully – our nicest white tablecloth, silver candlesticks, braided bread, silver cups (some filled with wine, some with grape juice), and a delicious-smelling meal.

We are ushering in the Jewish Sabbath with Kiddush.

The Kiddush prayer tells the story of God creating the world in six days and resting on the seventh. When we light the candles and sing Kiddush, we mark a shift – from mundane time to holy time – as we commit to resting on the seventh day too.

As I sit at the festive meal with my family and friends, I don't even consider checking e-mail or taking a phone call. Finally, after a busy workweek, I begin to relax. During the 24-hour period of the Sabbath, observant Jews disconnect 100% from anything even remotely related to work. And one thing I've noticed is that while the world goes on, it's never hard to catch up.

Friday night Kiddush is like "clocking in" the Sabbath time clock. Then, on Saturday night, another ceremony, called Havdallah (meaning separation), marks the end of the Sabbath. Havdallah is like "clocking out" the Sabbath time clock.

These time-based rituals are necessary because the Sabbath is a time-based experience unrelated to space. It's observed wherever you happen to be when the Sabbath starts.

In other words, physical walls are irrelevant. Instead, Jews rely on symbolic walls, marked not by stone but by ceremony, separating time from time, work from rest, mundane from holy.

Regardless of whether we go outside to a physical office, our physical work walls have collapsed.

That made me realize that I needed a marker – a ritual that punches my time clock – to delineate work from nonwork. A way to preserve who I am even in the midst of working hard to become who I want to be.

To acknowledge the start of my work day, I light a candle and say a short prayer asking for guidance and strength to act with integrity.

At the end of the day, I light a candle again, and, as I go over the day in my head, I will offer a prayer of thanks.

I won't "clock in" until after my children have left for school. And after I "clock out" I won't touch work until I light my candle the next morning. If you e-mail me after my prayer of thanks, I won't get the e-mail until my prayer for guidance the next morning.

If you want to do this with me, I would suggest that you perform your ritual religiously, though it doesn't have to be religious. It could be something you say to yourself, a song you listen to, time you take to write in your journal, a meditation, a mark on a piece of paper, an object you move, or anything that, for you, signifies a separation between work and not work.

After you have ritually left work, have the confidence to really leave it. Let your computer and phone idle while you live a little. And there's even a work upside too: You'll be fresher when you get back to work – more productive knowing you have to be because work will stop – and more creative as you integrate nonwork ideas into your work life.

A few days ago, I walked into Daniel and Sophia's room where Daniel was typing on a pretend laptop that Sophia had made out of construction paper.

"Hey Daniel, whatcha doin', buddy?" I asked him.

"One minute," he said to me as he continued to type without looking up from the paper computer, "I'm almost done."

I felt like laughing and crying at the same time.

"I'll wait," I finally said, "and when you're done, let's both shut our computers and put them away for the night, okay?"

Our lives depend on it.

How do we know we're on the right track? That we're confident in who we are while still growing into who we want to be? We need to measure our traction, of course. In the next chapter, I'd like to propose a novel metric ...

CHAPTER 12

HOW WILL YOU MEASURE SUCCESS?

WHY YOU SHOULD TREAT LAUGHTER AS A METRIC

I was following the same yoga video I had followed more than 30 times in the past. Because I know the routine well, I usually have little trouble breathing rhythmically through the postures, feeling the subtleties of each movement, and sliding gently into a mind-body meditation.

This time, though, was drastically off. Not only did my mind wander, I was clumsy and confused. I did "Warrior 1" twice on the same side instead of switching legs. I lost my balance in eagle pose. And, at one point, looking up at the video from my standing split, I found myself two postures behind the leader.

The worst part wasn't my poor performance though; it was my attitude and mood. I felt stressed, annoyed, and anxious – hardly the outcome I was looking for from yoga. It didn't support my sense of self; it was a confidence drag.

The problem? I wasn't only doing yoga. I was watching TV at the same time.

It was an experiment that I started after a conversation with my mother. She and I were talking about her dinner plans and she mentioned she was going out with a couple she really enjoys. I asked what she enjoyed about them.

"They laugh a lot," she answered, "and I love that. People don't laugh so much anymore."

Her comment stuck with me. She's right: We don't laugh as much as we used to.

As I thought more about it, I arrived at a hypothesis I chose to test: It's not that we're depressed, it's that we're distracted. And laughter, it turns out, is not something that happens when we're distracted.

There is clearly a productivity downside to multitasking. As my yoga experience and countless studies show, we pay a steep price in efficiency and productivity for spreading our attention so thinly.

But my mother's observation points to a more nefarious consequence of multitasking: its emotional impact.

It's impossible to feel joy or pleasure when our attention is fractured. Anger, frustration, annoyance – sure. Those emotions rise to the surface easily. In fact, multitasking encourages them. But laughter? It's nearly impossible.

Why is this important? Does it really matter whether we're laughing more or less? What does this have to do with leadership?

Everything, it turns out. My yoga experiment wasn't the first I'd tried. Before that, I watched television while processing my credit card bill on an Excel spreadsheet – a seemingly mindless task that involves nothing more than dragging numbers from one cell to another. Not only did it take four times as long as when I did it undistracted, but I grew increasingly irritated as I worked. When someone walked into my office with a question, I growled. I felt terrible about myself.

That's a confidence issue.

Not laughing is a symptom – a lagging indicator – of an ill that's creating havoc in our lives and our organizations.

We aren't laughing anymore because we aren't fully present anymore. Physically we're in one place but mentally, we're all over the place. Think about some recent phone conversations you've had – and then consider what else you were doing at the same time. Were you driving? Surfing the web? Reading and deleting e-mails? Shooting off a text? Sorting through mail? Or maybe you were thinking about any number of problems – a renovation, a recent argument, a never-ending to-do list – unrelated to the topic at hand.

Unfortunately, being fully present in the moment has become a casualty of our too full and harried lives.

"But don't some people get intense pleasure from the challenge of focusing on more than one thing at a time?" a friend asked me when I shared this notion with her. "What about complex multidimensional activities, like doing a presentation?"

She's right. I love doing presentations. And when I do a presentation, I'm thinking about innumerable things at once – the content, my delivery, the energy in the room, my timing for a joke, that person in the front row who seems disgruntled, the amount of minutes I have left, and so on.

But the reason I love the excitement of all those variables is precisely because they keep me laser-focused. I'm battle-ready, all my senses are alert, prepared for anything. Yes, I'm holding a lot of things at once, but they're all related. That builds confidence.

Complex multidimensional activities hold so much pleasure precisely because they require singular focus. Everything we're dealing with is connected. It's when we're focused simultaneously on things that are disconnected – like a conversation and an e-mail – that we struggle.

Here's the good news: The solution is fun.

As an achievement-driven guy, I'd like to suggest a personal challenge: Try to increase the number of times you laugh in a day. I don't mean chuckle – that's not a high enough bar – I mean really laugh. Choose a number: 3? 8? 20? Then try to achieve it.

On the surface, this seems a little nuts. But think about it: We measure all sorts of things in organizations that supposedly drive results; why not laughter? At least until we get the hang of it again.

The interesting thing about laughter is that you can't force it. It just happens when the conditions are right. And the conditions are right when you are comfortable in yourself, confident, settled, focused on what you're doing in the moment.

So how do we get our laughter numbers up? Create the conditions that make laughter more likely: Do one thing at a time. Focus on it entirely. If a distracting thought enters your mind and you're afraid of forgetting it, write it down for later when you can focus on it exclusively. Don't spread your attention beyond what's right in front of you right now.

And relax into all the things we've talked about in Element One: Build Your Confidence. Find your ground even when things swirl around you. Stay curious about, compassionate with, and appreciative of all parts of yourself. Get a clear view of your future and practice it, with gratitude for how amazing you already are. Invest your energy wisely and you will grow your confidence and become even more of who you want to be.

We already know those things will make us more productive and powerful people. It's nice to know they'll bring us joy and laughter too.

ELEMENT TWO

CONNECT WITH OTHERS

Build Your Confidence
- Know Who You Are
- Become Who You Want To Be

Connect with Others
- **Be Curious and Trusting**
- **Be Clear and Trustworthy**

Commit to Purpose
- Energize Your Focus
- Focus Their Energy

Cultivate Emotional Courage
- Feel Courageously
- Act Boldly

Your ability to move forward on important work is directly related to your ability to connect with others, inspire them, and motivate their action. The confidence you built in the last section has given you a solid foundation, a sense of self, and a future-focused orientation. That will help you connect with others from a place of strength, and keep you from losing yourself in the process. Your task here is to profoundly see and appreciate others – and to be profoundly seen and appreciated by them – thereby developing relationships that build loyalty and commitment in those around you. In the context of those very real relationships, you will learn to have hard conversations and make difficult decisions people may not always agree with, while *deepening* your connection to them.

Part One of this section, Be Curious and Trusting, deeply connects you with others, as you listen, learn, and support people. If you want people to trust you, you have to trust them first. The chapters in this part will help you build, and convey, your trust in the people around you. Your manager, colleagues, employees, clients – even your friends and family – will feel seen and heard, appreciated, and trusted. Your receptivity to others will translate into their loyalty and devotion.

Part Two of this section, Be Clear and Trustworthy, will introduce you to your superpower (you can change people's moods, feelings, and attitudes) and help you show up in a way that energizes the people around you. You will learn how to deliver messages clearly, powerfully, and compellingly. You'll be more willing to have the hard conversations you need to have, and you will be more trustworthy precisely because you are willing to have those hard conversations. When you do this, others will be far more likely to "buy in" to your vision. The chapters in this part are very practical with specific guidance about what to say and how to say it. The confidence you built in Element One, and the relationships you build in Part One of this section, will serve you well as you take responsibility for what's yours to own, and acknowledge the people around you for what they contribute. You will be clear and trustworthy.

PART ONE

BE CURIOUS AND TRUSTING

CHAPTER 13

THE IMPACT OF TRUST

THE REAL SECRET OF THOROUGHLY EXCELLENT COMPANIES

At a well-known five-star hotel, I asked if I could extend my checkout time by two hours. I was told no; the hotel was full. Unless I paid for a half day; then they'd accommodate me.

Huh?

If the hotel was full and needed my room, why would it make a difference if I paid them? And if they *did* have the ability to extend my checkout, why would they charge me? I spoke with the manager. Same answer.

That was the last time I stayed at that hotel franchise.

Contrast that to my recent experience at the Four Seasons in Dallas, Texas, a hotel where I've stayed several times.

When I arrived, I didn't have to stand in line to check in; the valet simply handed me the key to my room. The room was setup exactly as I like it: a yoga mat, an exercise schedule on the bed, and a bowl of fruit on the table. And they automatically extended my checkout time.

I am a customer for life.

How do they do it? What's their secret?

I sat down with Michael Newcombe, general manager of the hotel and 17-year veteran with the Four Seasons, to find out. A woman from room service brought us water and we began to talk.

He told me about meeting Isadore "Issy" Sharp, who founded the Four Seasons in 1960 and is still its CEO. Michael met Issy in London two weeks before transferring to a mid-level job at the Four Seasons in Toronto. Issy shook his hand and told him he'd check on him the week he arrived in Toronto. True to his word, Issy showed up that first week to make sure Michael was settling in comfortably.

Michael tells that story to all new hires on their first day.

Michael practices proximity management. Every month he meets informally with each employee group. No agenda. No speeches. Just conversation. That helps him solve problems: For example, the time guest check-in was being mysteriously delayed.

During his meeting with the front desk staff, he learned they were slower than usual in checking in guests because rooms weren't available. Then, in his meeting with housekeeping staff, someone asked if the hotel was running low on king size sheets. Most CEOs wouldn't be interested in that question, but Michael asked why. Well, the maid answered, it's taking us longer to turn over rooms because we have to wait for the sheets. So he kept asking questions to different employee groups until he discovered that one of the dryers was broken and waiting for a custom part. That reduced the number of available sheets. Which slowed down housekeeping. Which reduced room availability. Which delayed guests from checking in.

He fixed the problem in 24 hours. A problem he never would have known about without open communication with all his employees.

Michael walks the property regularly. He asks employees about their families, brings donuts, arranges birthday parties and softball tournaments. He gets beyond the nametag.

I tested him by asking about the woman who poured our water. He smiled, "Judith transferred here from Nevis four years ago, before I arrived at the hotel." And then he told me a little about her family.

These are all good management techniques. Perhaps the secret is that Michael does what others just talk about? But there's more to the hotel's approach.

To get a job at the Four Seasons, you need to make it through five interviews, each looking at you from a different angle. The HR director assesses your ability to work. The division head assesses your skills. The department head looks at cultural fit. The resort manager explores your potential to grow within the resort. And the GM (yes, Michael meets every new prospective employee) looks at your potential to move to another resort.

One in 20 new applicants gets through the process. A 5% admissions rate. That's more competitive than Harvard.

Each interviewer is looking for one thing. Together they get a full picture of an applicant. Can he do the job? Will he fit in? Can he grow? Perhaps that's the key to a turnover rate of 11% compared with the industry norm of 27%.

Almost as an afterthought, Michael mentioned one more thing. "When an employee transfers to another resort, they're accepted without interviewing."

"On the basis of?" I asked.

"Our recommendation."

And there it was. The secret ingredient.

Trust.

Sure it's important to stay close to employees, clients, and products. And it makes an important difference when the CEO listens and really cares.

But underlying these is trust, deeply embedded in the culture of the organization, exemplified in its daily operations, driving its success.

Trust is as simple as following through on your commitments. Every sales person knows the way to make a quick sale is to develop quick trust. A good sales person will send you an article with a little note saying it made her think of you. That builds a relationship.

But a great sales person will call you to tell you she saw an article that made her think of you and promise to send it to you. Then she'll send it. That builds trust.

Great sales people create an opportunity to fulfill a commitment — even when one doesn't naturally exist — and then fulfill it. Like Issy Sharp's promise to visit Michael in Toronto.

Michael listens to his employees and trusts they have something real to say. In turn, they trust him enough to say what's on their mind. Each interviewer looks for something different and trusts the viewpoint of the others. And each GM trusts the others to transfer only those employees who will succeed in the new resort.

I know plenty of managers who transfer their poor performers to other divisions. But at the Four Seasons that would kill a GM. They know their reputations depend on successful transfers.

That trust trickles down from GM to employees. And from employees to guests.

I was in the locker room, having just worked out in the gym and taken a shower. I didn't want to put my sweaty clothes back on, so I was wearing a gym bathrobe. I was worried the locker room attendant wouldn't want me taking a bathrobe out of the locker room. How could they keep track of the robes? Guests might take them home. That's why so many hotels have little notes on their robes that say, "You are welcome to buy this robe in our gift shop."

So I was walking out of the locker room in the robe, sweaty clothes in my arms, when the locker room attendant said, "Excuse me, sir."

Busted, I thought to myself, as I turned to face him.

"Would you like a bag to carry your gym clothes up to your room?" he asked, holding out a plastic laundry bag.

Trust.

It's not easy to trust people. It's a risk. It's why it requires emotional courage. But there are ways to make it easier. Things you can do that increase the likelihood that you will trust someone (and that they will be trustworthy), and deepen the connection between you. It's as easy – and hard – as staying open ...

CHAPTER 14

STAY OPEN

HOW TO REALLY LISTEN

One morning, my wife Eleanor woke up, turned over, and said, "I am not looking forward to this day." I asked her why.

What came out is that we were at the start of the Jewish high-holy-day season (again), which means colder weather and three weeks of big social meals, long religious services, broken routines, and children out of school. Eleanor didn't grow up with these traditions, and they can be overwhelming.

Now, I run a management consulting company; problem solving is what I do. So it didn't take me long to jump in.

"Cold weather means ski season is about to start," I said. "You love skiing. And these holiday meals are fun and filled with people you love – they'll make you feel better. And I'll be with you; you won't be alone with the kids. Also, you know, Jesus was Jewish, so it's kind of your tradition too."

Even as I said it, I knew that last one was a reach. It became clear that I was making her feel worse and now she wasn't just sad, she was angry.

And when she got angry, I felt myself get angry too. And self-righteous. Here I am trying to help her and this is what I get?

But then I smartened up. I remembered that what I most want with Eleanor is connection. I want that even more than I want to appear smart or solve her problems. So, instead of giving in to my anger, which would have really blown things up, I leaned into curiosity.

That is to say, I shut up and listened.

When I did, I began to hear the real stuff, the things that neither of us was actually saying.

What I discovered was that she was upset because the focus on mothers during the Jewish holidays taps into her insecurities about motherhood, not being a Jewish mom, and not having time to spend on her own work.

I also discovered that my own babbling wasn't so much to help her feel better as to help *me* feel better. I'm the reason she's in New York City, living through cold winters, and part of a Jewish family.

In other words, by trying to make her feel better, I was doing the opposite of making her feel better. I was arguing with her. In fact, most of the time when we try to make people feel better, we end up arguing with them because we're contradicting what they're feeling. Which, inevitably, makes them feel worse.

Listening, it turns out, is magic. It communicates not only my curiosity, but also my trust in her and her feelings. It helped me understand what was going on with both of us, and it helped Eleanor feel better, too. It made her feel that she wasn't alone in her feelings; I was with her. It deepened our connection.

But listening isn't easy. The more we listen to others, the more likely we will react – or overreact – to what they say. Which communicates a lack of curiosity and erodes trust.

Listening, it turns out, is much harder than speaking. We have to allow things we might disagree with to hang in the air. We have to move over a little and create space for those things to linger.

That kind of listening takes the confidence we've been building in the last section. And it takes tremendous courage.

But if we're interested in learning – about ourselves as well as others – then it's worth it. And if we're interested in being connected to others, showing them respect, helping them feel better, and solving problems between us, then it's more than worth it. It's essential.

Until people feel heard, they will fight to be heard. But once they are heard, there is little left to fight for, and then we can move on, not as "us vs. them" but simply as "us."

So how do you listen in a way that conveys trust and curiosity?

1. **Actually listen.** And only listen. That means don't multi-task. I'm not just talking about doing e-mail, surfing the web, or creating a grocery list. Thinking about what you're going to say next counts as multitasking. Simply focus on what the other person is saying.

2. **Repeat back.** This feels a little silly at first but works magic. If someone says she is angry about the decision you just made, you can say "you're angry about the decision I just made." I know, I know, she just said that. But it shows you're listening and it communicates to the other person that she's been heard. If you don't have the courage to try it with an adult, try it with a child. You'll see what a difference it makes and it will embolden you to try it with a colleague or your spouse.

3. **Ask questions.** Explore the other person's thoughts and feelings more deeply. And "You don't really believe that, do you?" does not count as a question. You are not using the Socratic method to prove your point; you are trying to better understand what's going on so you can better understand your partner in this conversation.

Really listening can feel risky, which seems strange because listening doesn't materially change anything. But sometimes you'll hear things that are hard to hear.

This might make it a little easier: Remember that listening is not the same thing as agreeing. And it will never force you to take any particular action. If anything, it will reduce the intensity of people's insistence that you take a specific action. Because in many cases what they're looking for is proof that you've heard them. So if they feel you've really heard them, their need for action diminishes.

As Eleanor spoke, I noticed my own resistance to various things she was saying. There's no question that it's hard to really listen. That's why it takes – and builds – emotional courage. But once I relaxed into it, I heard her in a much deeper way. That made her feel better. Call me codependent, but it made me feel better too.

It turns out that sometimes, just listening *is* problem solving. People want you to trust and be curious about them. When you are, they feel received and connected to you. Listening to them is one way to do that. Seeing them in all their complexity is another ...

CHAPTER 15

STAY CURIOUS ABOUT OTHERS

PEOPLE CAN'T BE SUMMED UP BY PERSONALITY TESTS

When we were in college, Eleanor, who was my girlfriend at the time, wanted me to take a personality assessment that would categorize me into one of 16 boxes, each box containing four letters that would explain me.

I didn't want to do it.

So she made it easy for me. "Come on, it'll be fun," she said. "I'll read the questions. You just lie there and answer. I'll write down your answers."

She began asking me questions, "Do you prefer to be with a group of people, or to be one-on-one?"

"I'd rather be one-on-one," I answered confidently.

"No way!" she replied, "You love being the center of attention. I'm checking a big YES."

She must have changed at least half my answers. I'm not saying she was wrong. Most of the time, I think we were both right.

By definition, personality assessments simplify complexity. That's not always a bad thing; putting a label on something helps us recognize it quickly. It's shorthand. And, given that most of us have more to do than we have time for, shorthand is useful.

But not with people. People are not easy to understand, and – here's where I disagree with the assessments – *they shouldn't be.*

People are too interesting and too complicated to be summed up in a simple assessment. Are there really only 16 basic personality types? Have you met my uncle Ralph? There are *at least* 17.

I would argue that no personality assessment is valid or reliable. These tests identify a black and white version of people, a reduction of who they really are. They offer us the illusion of understanding at the cost of truth and freedom. Sure, they may make people more comfortable ("Oh, I understand you now"). But it's a trick.

Self-assessments, by definition, reinforce a person's self-image. You tell the assessment who you think you are, and then the assessment tells you who you are. Which, of course, would incline you to think they're valid. But they're just telling you what you just told them.

Personality tests reinforce our blind spots. How would you respond to the statement: *You put every minute to good use?* Personally, I would answer "no." But Eleanor would say that I use my time incredibly productively. What's the truth? Here's another way of asking the question: Who knows me better, Eleanor or me? The truth is somewhere in between. She sees things I don't. I know things she doesn't.

I want to suggest an alternative. A tool that is far more reliable at understanding the complexity of a human being. A tool that is practically infallible, almost always truthful, and surprisingly practical. A tool that not only helps you understand other people but simultaneously improves your relationships with them, communicates your trust in them, and helps you learn, in real time, how to communicate with them, even in – especially in – the face of conflict or disagreement.

That tool? Curiosity.

As soon as we label something, our curiosity about that thing diminishes. Personality assessments are a shortcut to getting to: "I know." And once we know something, we're no longer curious.

But that's not nearly as powerful as living in the mindset of "I don't know." True understanding comes from *not* knowing. Real connection comes from *not* knowing. Brilliant innovation and problem solving comes from *not* knowing.

See people. Don't label them. Allow yourself to be surprised. Notice how someone may be different today than yesterday. How someone's personality – or point of view – may change when you eat lunch together instead of meeting in their office. Notice how often communication "tactics" actually get in the way of communication.

Recently one of our clients asked us to lead a session in which each person on the team would take a character strength self-assessment. I have often seen teams and organizations use assessments like this (e.g., let's put everyone's strengths and weaknesses on the table so we can support each other).

I proposed a different idea. Together, as a team, they should agree on the three to five most important character traits that would help the team achieve its objectives (instead of the 24 character traits assessed by the instrument). Then, in small groups, they should give feedback to each other about those character traits and talk about what they can do to take advantage of their strengths and mitigate their weaknesses.

To do this, they would have to learn how to talk about sensitive issues, how to listen without getting defensive, and how to share, courageously, what they perceive in each other.

That's the point. Not only will they gain the benefit of the information, they will increase their capability to have difficult conversations. It's those conversations, not the assessments, that will improve relationships and results in an organization.

If you want to understand people, talk to them. Ask questions. Listen to their answers and to the silence between their answers. Watch their body language. Study them. And stay open to what you may find about them and about yourself.

Here's one thing you'll find: People are constantly changing. If you talk to someone in a meeting and then, a little while later, over a bite to eat, you may notice that his personality completely shifts. Curiosity allows you to see people more clearly and learn about them in all their beautiful and interesting variability. And because of that, it helps you build much stronger, more resilient relationships.

If you've based your relationship on curiosity, when you have to communicate about something difficult, you'll be talking to a person, not an ENTJ (one of the boxes in the Myers–Briggs type personality assessment). You'll be more understanding – and a lot more convincing.

But it's hard to let go of the comfort that comes from thinking you've figured someone out.

I was leading a two-day training for senior-level coaches who were interested in working for my firm. Coaches love assessments and many of the coaches in the room were certified to administer a gaggle of them. During the training, I made it very clear that, at Bregman Partners, we don't use personality assessments for all the reasons I stated earlier. I told the coaches that one of our hallmarks is that we remain curious and we encourage our clients to remain curious, which makes them much stronger leaders.

After the training, one of the coaches came up to me.

"You're an ENFP," she told me.

"Seriously?" I was bewildered. "Have you been listening?"

"I teach Myers–Briggs," she said, "And I've been watching you all day. I'm telling you, you're an ENFP. I know you don't like these tests, but I think you don't understand them."

"I don't think that's the problem," I answered, "The problem is they think they understand me."

Even more than a skill, curiosity is a way of being in the world. Curiosity asks us to stay – often longer than is comfortable – in the place of *not knowing*. Being willing to "not know" will, counterintuitively, help you understand others even better. Staying curious is the only way we will learn something new – not just about people, but about problems too …

CHAPTER 16

STAY CREATIVE

ARE YOU TRYING TO SOLVE THE WRONG PROBLEM?

"That's my shirt, Sophia. Take it off!"

"Daniel! Get off my bed!"

"Isabelle, get out of the bathroom!"

It was 6:45 a.m. and my three kids were already fighting.

Eleanor and I have tried everything. We talked to them about how important it is to have a good relationship with your siblings, made clear what we expected, and developed rules for living together. We trained them in respectful communication and taught them how to breathe and manage their anger. We meditated with them and mediated between them. We rewarded them, punished them, reasoned with them, and begged them.

Still, here they were, fighting. Again. And now I was about to lose my temper. Which, of course, never helps.

What do you do when you have a sticky problem involving others, that you've attempted to solve in every way possible and none of your solutions have worked?

In the organizational coaching we do at Bregman Partners, we see situations like these daily because they are precisely the kind of situations people bring to coaches: problems that seem unresolvable, involving other people, that stall forward momentum. For example, an employee who doesn't take accountability. You've spoken about accountability and maybe you've even gotten angry a few times when the work did not meet your expectations. Still, nothing you do seems to have an impact. How can curiosity and trusting them help?

Here's a strategy that almost never works – come up with yet another solution you haven't tried or tell them to just try harder. More than anything, that simply communicates that you don't trust that they're trying hard enough.

A strategy that almost always works? Solve a different problem.

I'm not saying you should give up on getting the result you want. What I am saying is that if you've tried to solve a problem with every solution you can think of, your challenge isn't finding a better solution. It's finding a better problem. And that's where curiosity can help.

If my kids didn't have a sibling-fighting problem, what else might it be? I thought through a number of different possibilities and landed on what turned out to be a simple problem with a very simple solution.

My kids didn't have a sibling problem; they had a morning problem. They woke up tired and with low blood sugar.

Which means the solution wasn't to teach them how to speak nicely to each other. In fact, that just exacerbated the problem because after we lectured them, they felt worse and now they weren't just mad at each other, they were mad at us.

The real solution? An earlier bedtime and a glass of orange juice when they woke up.

Those two interventions decreased the morning fighting by 90%.

The reason a coach – or any outside perspective – is helpful in these sticky problems is not because the coach is smarter or has more creative solutions. It's because insiders don't question the problem definition the way an outsider does. Being outside the system helps us see the system in a way that insiders can't see.

If you are caught in a problem that seems unsolvable, ask this simple question: If you trusted that the other person was doing their best to solve the problem as you and they see it, what else might the problem be?

In other words, rather than point your curiosity toward the solution, try pointing it toward the problem.

The employee who isn't taking accountability no matter what you've tried? Consider that maybe accountability isn't his problem. Perhaps it's capability. Or unclear communication of expectations. Or lack of objective measurement. If any of those are the problems, then a whole new set of solutions will present themselves.

There's an additional advantage to redefining your problem: It frees you to experiment with "beginner's mind." You get to start over, trying different solutions, assessing their effectiveness, learning from failures, and trying again.

To address your employee's accountability gap, try being crystal clear with expectations. If that doesn't shift anything, try some training that might increase his capability. Involving your employee in figuring out the problem has the added advantage of deepening engagement, which may affect performance all on its own.

With my kids, I asked them whether they thought they might have a morning problem instead of a sibling one. They agreed to experiment with the orange juice and were delighted when we served it to them in bed.

They still wake up grumpy. But here's how I know we're solving the right problem: Their moods radically change within minutes of eating or taking a few sips of orange juice.

In other words, I know we're solving the right problem because the solution works.

In the past few chapters, we've looked at ways of connecting with others by being curious and trusting in situations where you have some control. But what about when you have no control? The best way to convey your curiosity and trust is to discover a way to be useful ...

CHAPTER 17

BE USEFUL

HOLD THE BABY

"Ladies and gentlemen, this is your Captain speaking. We have a situation." And with those words, the saga of my aborted flight from New York to Dallas began.

The captain told us we had an "equipment problem" that required we make an emergency landing at Washington Dulles, the nearest airport. But, he continued, the plane was too heavy to land safely; we had to shed fuel. So we would fly around in a circle for 45 minutes and land as soon as we were light enough.

I was sitting at the front of the plane and made eye contact with the flight attendant.

"What's the problem?" I mouthed.

"I don't know," she responded with the hint of a shrug, "they won't tell us."

"If we're going to fly for 45 minutes, can't he fly toward Dallas instead of in circles?" I asked. She smiled and looked down.

So we circled. If you had taken a picture of us before the announcement and another one after, you would have had difficulty telling the difference. People were reading, listening to music, talking softly.

But in fact, everything had changed. Our level of anxiety had skyrocketed. We were on a plane that was stuck in the air, unable to land but apparently unsafe to fly for a reason none of us but the pilot knew, and there was nothing we could do about it.

It occurred to me how psychologically similar this circumstance was to so many others we experience. We were stuck in a situation in which we are not in control and cannot immediately escape. Like the economy or, at times, our company or our team.

This plane was a lab and we were the rats. How do we respond when we are stuck, vulnerable, nervous, and have no positional power?

Unfortunately there was nothing to observe. What I needed was a stimulus. Something to bring people's reactions to the surface. Something like ... a screaming baby.

The baby in the seat behind me generously accommodated. He let out a sharp cry, followed by waves of wailing. His mother tried to soothe him – shushing, gently tapping on his back – but the screeching only got louder.

Let the games begin.

Sitting across the aisle from the mother was a woman, probably in her 60s who became increasingly annoyed. She glared. Sighed loudly. And finally, in a "whisper" to her seatmate that was clearly meant to be heard said, "Can't that woman control her baby?" Her seatmate smiled awkwardly without looking up from her magazine.

"I think I've figured out what's wrong." The man sitting next to me who had been staring out the window now turned to face me. "It's a problem with the wheels. They just let the gear down and we're way higher than 1,000 feet. Must be a problem with the landing gear." He proceeded to talk to me about the mechanics of an airplane and what would happen in a crash landing with inoperative wheels.

I turned to look down the aisle just in time to see one woman cry out, say something about the baby, and beat her magazine on the back of the seat in front of her. Unfortunately for the man sitting there, she hit him on the head. When he turned in utter surprise, she started babbling out an apology. I kid you not.

There were, of course, many others – most people on the plane – who didn't have any observable reaction.

Then something magical happened. The woman sitting next to the mother offered to hold the baby for a few moments, to provide the mother a little relief. I turned in time to see the mother smile — it didn't appear that they knew each other — pass the baby, thank her profusely, and shut her eyes. The baby continued to cry, but everyone else settled down a bit.

In a few short minutes I'd observed many of the common reactions to frustration during stress. Although each of the responses might be psychologically useful, one came out the clear winner. What would life be like if more of us offered to hold the baby?

Someone on your team is consistently unprepared at meetings. You're not the leader so you can't declare it unacceptable. What do you do? You could complain to others or roll your eyes or try to ignore it. That might make you feel better in the moment, but it would reflect your lack of curiosity and trust, disconnecting you from your colleague.

Alternatively, you could hold the baby: Partner with him on a project, offer to prepare with him, or share ideas before the next meeting. Those solutions communicate trust and openness in a way that builds connection.

One of your colleagues is overworked, stressed, seemingly unproductive, and making your team look bad. On top of that, she's constantly complaining about how much harder her job is than yours. Annoying, right? You'd be justified in gossiping about her or simply letting her fail. But what if you offered to help? Maybe even stayed late one night working with her?

Your company comes out with a new technology initiative that seems to make everyone's lives more complicated. Yet they say it's necessary. It's so easy to complain about it. Or to nod along with others when they complain about it. But what if you learned enough about it to help the people who were struggling with it?

In situations in which we may have no positional authority — we're not the leader, we don't have all the information, we can't make the decisions, we aren't in control — we still have power: the power to influence our own experience and, sometimes, the experiences of others. Holding the baby gives us something useful to do. It makes us and others feel good. It might even help solve the problem. What's important to remember is that it's always a choice.

Finally, 35 minutes after his first announcement, the Captain told us we had been cleared to land. I looked out the window and saw the flashing lights of ambulances and fire trucks lining the runway. The man next to me, having already described all the possible ways we might die, gave me a *see, I told you it was bad* look. I tightened my seat belt.

The wheels touched the ground. Nobody moved. Would the plane stop? The engines roared and the plane slowed. Everyone burst into applause. We had landed gently and easily.

Our saga, and my experiment, was over.

Then the airline representative explained the procedures for getting rebooked on another flight, and people started jockeying for a place on line and speaking loudly on cell phones to their travel agents. One woman started to plead for a spot on the next flight. People around her started to roll their eyes.

Let the games begin (again).

In all the chapters in this part, we've been talking about using curiosity and trust to connect more deeply with others by hearing, seeing, trusting, appreciating, and helping them. That's a lot, and it's easy to miss the mark (as I learned the hard way). That's where attunement can help ...

CHAPTER 18

MAKE PEOPLE FEEL GOOD

HOW NOT TO LOSE A SALE

Robyn, a close friend of mine, and a senior leader at a large pharmaceutical company, referred me to work with Dan, the CEO of one of her company's subsidiaries and someone she knew well. She would arrange for the three of us to meet. The lead wasn't just warm; it was hot.

During the sales process I made a series of decisions, all of which felt – in fact, still feel – eminently reasonable. Here's what happened:

1. With Dan's permission, Robyn and I met several times before the meeting to discuss Dan and his situation. Dan was new to his role as CEO and needed to step up in tricky circumstances. By the time I met with him, I understood his challenges and it was clear that they fit squarely in my sweet spot as an advisor.

2. The day of the meeting, Robyn and Dan were running behind schedule. We had planned for 60 minutes but now only had 20. "No problem," I told them, "I've been briefed about the situation, so we can cut to the chase."

3. I sat down in an empty office chair that happened to be uncomfortably low to the ground and I instinctively raised the seat to the level at which I normally sit.

4. Dan started the conversation with a compliment about my latest book and told me how much he enjoyed my blog posts, which reinforced my decision to "cut to the chase."

5. I explained briefly what I knew about his situation and when he acknowledged that I understood it, I launched into how I would approach it.

6. At one point, Dan asked me a question and I hesitated before answering. Robyn suggested that we discuss it later but I didn't want to disappoint so I thanked her but said I'd be happy to share my thoughts and I did.

Nothing I did, said, thought, or felt was dramatically off base. In fact, each step – each choice I made – was practical, sensible, and appropriate from my perspective.

That is precisely why I crashed.

I was operating from my perspective. But Dan wasn't. He was operating from his perspective. And from his perspective, the fact that I was operating from my perspective was a deal-breaker.

The problem? I wasn't attuned.

Daniel Pink, in his excellent book *To Sell Is Human: The Surprising Truth About Moving Others,* calls attunement one of the three most valuable qualities you need to move others.

Essentially, attunement is being in sync with who's and what's around you. When you're in attunement, you're *curious.* You ask questions, you listen to the answers, and you empathize.

I might have been attuned to the challenges Dan was facing – but everything I did and said indicated that I wasn't attuned to Dan. Or even to Robyn.

According to Pink, the first rule of attunement is to reduce your power. You do that by letting go of your perspective, which opens space for you to share the perspective of others. Pink quoted one highly successful salesperson who related this to humility. Great sales people, she said, take the attitude, "I'm sitting in the small chair so you can sit in the big chair."

I did the opposite. I raised my seat, literally and figuratively. I took control of the conversation, sidelined Robyn when she suggested we talk later, and spent what little time I had trying to prove to Dan that I understood it all and I was the right guy to help.

I was all clarity, no curiosity. I showed lots of trust in myself, but very little in Dan and Robyn.

I was too easily flattered by Dan's comment about my book, too rushed by our time crunch, and too eager to impress both Robyn and Dan. I tried so hard to prove my competence that I came off as incompetent. Maybe not in terms of my solution, but certainly in terms of our relationship.

I acted with the sensibility of an extrovert, which is typically assumed to offer a strong sales advantage. But Pink's research suggests that being extroverted can actually be a liability. Why? Because too often we talk when we should be listening.

To the extent that I listened at all, I was listening to gather enough information so I could make a case to Dan that I could solve his problem. In other words, I wasn't listening out of curiosity, I was listening simply to empower my speaking.

But why didn't that work? Wasn't Dan looking for information about me and what I might do for him?

Maybe. But he as much as told me he knew enough about me from my writing, just as I knew a lot about him from my conversations with Robyn. No, Dan didn't really want to hear me speak. He wanted to hear me listen.

What Dan was really looking to figure out – what most people are looking to figure out – is what it would feel like to work together. And what I showed him in our brief conversation is that it would feel like some expert coming in and telling him what he should do.

If I were Dan, I wouldn't hire me either.

What would I do differently next time? I would sit in the chair I was offered and listen to Dan tell his story. Then I would ask him a number of questions to make sure I could see the situation with his eyes, analyze it from his point of view, and feel his emotions. I would attune to him.

That would require that I let go of my agenda, stop trying to get hired, give up trying to quickly and smartly summarize what Dan needed, and cease trying to prove myself.

My goal, the entire purpose of my presence, would be to connect.

If I did that well, I wouldn't have to worry about showing him what I was capable of. There would be plenty of time for that later – once we started working together.

PART TWO

BE CLEAR AND TRUSTWORTHY

CHAPTER 19

EVERYONE IS CONTAGIOUS

HOW TO USE YOUR SUPERPOWER FOR GOOD

I folded my bike and carried it into the lobby of the office building in midtown Manhattan. The security guard behind the desk looked up at me, grimaced, then looked down again and growled something indecipherable.

"Excuse me?" I asked.

He sighed loudly and didn't say anything for a moment. Then, without bothering to look at me, he said, "You're not coming in here with that."

I was already jittery because of a near miss with a taxi on the ride over, and this deflated me even more. It wasn't his message – I've faced many security guards who don't like to permit bicycles into their buildings – it was his cold, disdainful tone.

I tried to stay calm and upbeat. I showed him how small it was, folded. I told him I had a bag I could put it in. He repeated the same line.

Finally, after citing the Bicycle Access to Office Buildings Law, which requires New York City buildings with freight elevators to admit bicycles, he let me in.

When I made it to the freight elevator, I smiled at the operator who was joking with some construction workers. He looked at me then looked back at his friends and kept talking. I waited uncomfortably for several minutes, and then asked him if he would take me to the nineteenth floor. He said something rude to his friends about tenants, took me up in silence, and left me in a small vestibule with a locked door but no clear way to enter.

He shut his door as I was asking him how to get in. "Try pushing the button," he barked through the closed elevator door. I saw the button he meant and pushed. At this point I was feeling lower than low.

Then, like magic, my morning changed.

"Hi! You must be Peter. Welcome!" Lisa, the receptionist, sang as she opened the door. She smiled, and then looked worried. "Why did you come up in the freight?"

I explained my morning and she frowned empathetically. "I'm so sorry, that's terrible. Here, let me take your bike."

I could have cried from happiness. In one second, Lisa turned my emotions around, from the negative spiral of anger, frustration, and despair to the positive spiral of relief, appreciation, and happiness.

And that's when I realized: We all have superpowers.

We can make people feel good or bad by as simple a thing as a gesture, an expression, a word, or a tone of voice.

But wait. Can I really blame my grumpiness on you? Isn't each person responsible for his or her own mood?

Here's what we know: Like the common cold, emotions are contagious. Caroline Bartel at New York University and Richard Saavedra at the University of Michigan studied 70 work groups across a variety of industries and found that people who worked together ended up sharing moods, good and bad. Moods converge.

This is particularly important to understand for people in positions of authority because leaders, more than anyone, set and spread the mood. If you've ever worked in an office, you know this from experience. If the boss is in a bad mood, conflicts increase. If she's in a good mood, people lighten up.

Does that mean we aren't responsible if we snap at someone in the hallway? That it's really the fault of the guy who bumped into us on the subway and didn't apologize?

Look at it this way: If you catch a cold from someone, does that mean you can go around sneezing on everyone else? You might be able to blame your mood on someone else, but you're still responsible for what you pass to others.

Nevertheless, it's hard to completely avoid infecting others when you have a cold. Several years ago I was asked to coach Renée, a senior manager in a retail company, who was receiving feedback that she was too harsh with her employees. She often raised her voice, criticized them mercilessly for mistakes, and humiliated them for not knowing things.

When I spoke to others in the office, I found out that the CEO to whom Renée reported treated his direct reports the same way. He was short-tempered, yelled a lot, and demanded perfection from others.

That didn't make it okay for Renée to treat her direct reports that way; it just made it harder for her not to.

That is a problem for the business because mood affects performance. According to research done by Sigal Barsade at Yale University, positive moods improved cooperation, decreased conflict, and increased performance.

So what's the solution?

Know your emotions, be in touch with your moods, and think of them like the common cold. If you feel infected by bad cheer, take a deep breath, recognize how you're feeling, and choose not to pass it on.

Instead, treat people with the empathy, care, and good humor that will make them feel happier, more connected, and more productive.

Here's the good news: Barsade's research found that positive moods are just as contagious as negative moods.

Is it really a choice though? If you're in a bad mood, can you decide to be happy? I find it hard, maybe inauthentic, even dishonest, to feign happiness.

But I have found a pretty simple solution to turning it all around: Kindness.

No matter how bad a mood I'm in, I've found it pretty straightforward to treat others with kindness. And that, invariably, has a positive affect on those around me, which, as we've seen, has a positive affect on me. And, voilà, my mood changes for the better.

When Lisa brought me to my client's office, I told him how my ugly morning had been turned around by his delightful receptionist. He responded with a story of his own. Once, when Lisa was sick and couldn't come to work, a quiet and reserved man named Frank, acted as receptionist for the day. Frank was not the sing-song type.

But he was used to Lisa's good cheer. Each morning, like everyone else in the office, he received her buoyant e-mails welcoming people to the office. And, on this particular day, when he was asked to fill in for Lisa, the mere memory of her lighthearted emotions was enough to influence Frank.

First thing that morning, on his own initiative, Frank wrote an e-mail to the whole office that read: "It's Pizzaaaaaaa for lunch! I hope everybody has a Happy Day!!!!!!"

And that is how you use your superpower for good.

Engaging people around positive, happy things is a good place to start. What about when you have to engage people around difficult topics? Here's how to talk about something you dread ...

CHAPTER 20

USE FEAR AS A GUIDE

HOW TO TALK ABOUT WHAT YOU MOST DREAD

"I have a question," a woman we'll call Tricia said to me during the break at a leadership training class I was teaching, "and I'd rather not ask it in front of everyone." "Everyone" being her colleagues, the other heads of departments at a financial services company.

We stepped outside the classroom. "It's my number two person, Joe," she told me. "He's a good performer but he's constantly taking credit for things, and goes overboard to try to get visibility. He thinks he's a team player but it doesn't feel that way to me or others in the group."

Hmmm, I wondered, why is she hesitant to talk about this in front of the others? Then, almost as an afterthought, she added, "I think he's after my job."

Oh.

There are two issues here:

1. Joe hogging credit and visibility.
2. Tricia's fear that Joe is gunning for her job.

Normally Tricia would have no problem talking to Joe about the first issue. It's the second issue that makes the first one hard to discuss. The negative fantasy goes like this: If I talk about Joe's ambitions

I might put the idea in people's heads. My boss and peers might start to think, "Hey, you know what? Maybe Joe should have her job." She's also afraid that she'll come off as insecure and weak.

Tricia's not alone. We face this double whammy all the time. You bungle a project but don't talk about it because you fear you'll get fired. You're overworked but hesitate to raise it because you worry about exposing your lack of capability. You're concerned a client isn't getting enough value but resist mentioning it because you're afraid you might lose the client.

The first issue – the bungled project, the overwork, the client's possible dissatisfaction – is public, professional, observable, and matter of fact. If you want to be clear and trustworthy, it needs to be discussed.

The second issue – the fear – is private, personal, emotional, and often, paralyzing.

Tricia doesn't *know* that Joe's after her job, she just senses and dreads it. No one *knows* he'll get fired for a bungled project so ignoring it seems safer than addressing it. But, of course, it's the opposite. When you go into denial and ignore something, you don't act. And if you don't act, you can't prevent what you fear from happening. In fact, your inaction may even make it more likely.

Here's a general rule: The more you fear a conversation, the more you probably need to have it. Think of fear as an indicator of a problem that needs to be addressed.

So how do you talk about your fear, dread, insecurity, and foreboding? You don't.

If Tricia raised her concerns about Joe wanting her job, he would immediately deny the accusation and, in so doing, make her feel foolish for raising it. They'd both leave the conversation with less trust in each other than before. Raising your suspicions about someone's negative intentions is almost always a bad idea.

But if you don't talk about your fear and you don't ignore your fear, what should you do? Sink your teeth into it.

"Tricia, I want you to make an assumption." I told her, "Assume that Joe is after your job. Why wouldn't he be? He's ambitious and you're in the job that would be his next step. It's a reasonable assumption."

In other words, assume the worst case. Assume your job is at risk. Assume you lack capability. Assume your client is planning to leave. Let's make it even worse: Assume everyone else knows it, too.

The sooner you accept the situation, the sooner you can do something about it. Instead of shying away from the answers, dive in. Remember: Use the fear as a catalyst, not a focus. Your focus needs to be the underlying problem. If you think your boss wants to fire you because of that last project you bungled, ask him to debrief the project and help you plan the next one. If you're worried that raising the issue of overwork will expose your lack of capability, talk to your boss about increasing your capability to manage the workload. An at-risk client? Let the client know you understand why they might be at risk of defection. Then listen. That makes you clear *and* trustworthy.

We often avoid conversations that make us feel vulnerable. Things that touch us deeply, our fears, our self-image, our future. But here's the thing: Not talking about them is what actually makes us vulnerable. Once we confront the underlying issues – say them out loud, ask about them, explore them – we feel, and become, much stronger, much less vulnerable. And then we can take powerful action.

So, how to deal with dread?

1. Notice it.
2. Understand the underlying problem it's signaling.
3. Talk openly about the problem, not the dread.
4. Fix the problem.

"Fine," Tricia responded, "I can see why it would be reasonable for him to want my job. But I'm not ready to leave, and he's not ready to step into it either. How do I fix the problem?"

"Help him fulfill his ambitions." I said, "Try it with me."

"Okay," she said. "Joe, you're smart and capable and a strong performer. My job – when you're ready – could be a good next step for you but I'm not going anywhere for now. What else interests you and how can I help you get there? I'd like to help you grow – whether it's here or even if it means going to another company."

"Great," I told her. "Then you can also talk about what might get in his way. That whether he wants your job or another, taking sole credit when others deserve some is a bad idea. And you can help him perform even better. As an ally. And from a position of strength, not as someone threatened by Joe, but as someone who can help him achieve his goals."

"Sounds easy," Tricia said

"It's not. Not if you're still afraid."

She laughed. "Afraid of what?"

Still, deciding to have the conversation – even having a plan for it – is easier than actually *having* it. Knowing how to start a hard conversation in a clear and trustworthy way will make it much easier (and more successful) ...

CHAPTER 21

LEAD WITH THE PUNCHLINE

HOW TO START A HARD CONVERSATION

I anticipated that the conversation would be difficult.

Shari and I had worked together for many years, and I knew she was expecting me to hire her to run a leadership program for one of my clients, Ganta, a high-tech company. But I didn't think Shari was the right fit for Ganta or, frankly, for the role of running the leadership training. In fact, I had become increasingly critical of her recent performance, though I hadn't mentioned anything to her about it yet.

That was my first mistake. I should have said something before it got to this point.

So why didn't I? I'd love to claim that it was because I liked her, and I didn't want to hurt her feelings. Or because I hoped things would get better without my intervention.

And while those things were true, there was a deeper truth: I was afraid of the cringe moment.

Do you know that uneasy moment, right as you're saying something that feels risky, but before the person responds? That's the cringe moment.

In other words, I delayed speaking with Shari because I was afraid of how I would feel giving her the negative feedback: awkward, uncomfortable, and maybe even unreasonable.

But I couldn't avoid it anymore. And because I had waited so long, the conversation promised to be even more awkward and uncomfortable. And now that she was getting a more extreme message with no warning, I would feel – and appear – even more unreasonable. The cringe quotient had gone up.

The day of the difficult conversation, I felt anxious as Shari came into my office. We shared a few pleasantries and then I began. I told her that I knew she wanted to run the leadership program at Ganta. I talked to her about the complexities and challenges of the leadership program and of Ganta in general. And I spoke with her about my frustrations with her recent performance. She asked me questions and I offered explanations and examples.

I did such a good job avoiding the cringe moment that, 30 minutes into the conversation, I still had not clearly communicated to Shari whether I was firing her or hiring her. My build-up was equally appropriate as context for either. I was completely unclear.

Finally, she did it for me. "So," she asked, "Are you saying that you don't want me to lead this program or you do?"

Now that I'm aware of it, I see my own behavior in leaders everywhere. Standing in front of the room, one senior VP slowly constructed a case to close a business. But he never got to his conclusion as people began debating unimportant details related to his argument before they even knew where he was headed.

In another case, a CEO sat in a meeting of department heads with the intention of telling them she was creating a new position to which they would all report. But she lost them as she spent the first 20 minutes giving context to a decision she hadn't yet announced. As one person later told me, "All of the context was lost on me as I was trying to guess what she was getting at. It was a complete waste of time."

The intellectual reason we build a case or give context to a difficult decision before announcing it is because we want to convey that the decision is well-thought-out, rational, and an inevitable conclusion to the facts. But since the listeners don't know what decision is being made, they have no context for the context and it all feels meaningless.

The irony is that our attempt to be clear is precisely what is getting in the way of our being clear.

The emotional reason we give such long introductions to hard decisions is because we are procrastinating. We're delaying the cringe feeling.

But this delay is counterproductive; it only stretches and deepens the discomfort of everyone involved.

The solution is simple and straightforward: Lead with the punchline.

What should I have said to Shari? "Thanks for coming in, Shari. I am not going to have you run the leadership program with Ganta, and I'd like you to understand why ... "

The senior VP should have started by saying, "I have come to the conclusion that we should close XXX business."

And the CEO should have opened her meeting with the department heads by declaring, "I have created a new Senior Vice President role, reporting to me, who will oversee this part of the business."

After those openings, people will be interested in hearing the rest. Or, they may surprise you with instant agreement and there may be little more to discuss.

Here's what I've come to realize: I almost always overestimate how difficult it is for the other person to hear what I have to say. People are resilient. I'm usually more uncomfortable delivering a difficult message than the other person is receiving it.

Next time you have a conversation you're dreading, lead with the part you're dreading. Get to the conclusion in the first sentence. Cringe fast and cringe early. It's a simple move that few of us make consistently because it requires emotional courage. At least the first time.

However, the more you do it, the easier and more natural it becomes. Being direct and upfront does not mean being callous or unnecessarily harsh. In fact, it's the opposite; done with care, being direct is far more considerate. It's clear and trustworthy. Perhaps surprisingly, it often deepens your connection with others, even if they are not happy with your conclusion.

And it doesn't just reduce angst, it saves time as well. Shari wasn't happy about not running the program at Ganta, but she understood why and accepted the decision quickly. Much more quickly than it took me to introduce it to her.

Now let's up the ante once again. How about being clear and trustworthy when you're in the heat of the moment? ...

CHAPTER 22

SKILLFUL COMMUNICATION IN THE HEAT OF THE MOMENT

OUTSMART YOUR NEXT ANGRY OUTBURST

Robert and Howard had always gotten along well. They'd worked on several projects together and considered each other friends. So when Robert discovered that Howard held a strategy meeting and hadn't included him, he felt betrayed. He immediately shot off a text to Howard: "I can't believe you didn't include me in that meeting!"

Howard was in the middle of a client meeting when his phone pinged with a new text. Stealing a look at his phone, he felt a jumble of things: concern, anger, embarrassment, frustration, defensiveness. The text distracted Howard, and his meeting didn't go as well as he had hoped. His anger grew as he thought about the fact that in a meeting earlier that week, Robert didn't support an idea Howard proposed to Jane, their CEO, even though before the meeting he'd said he liked the idea. So as soon as Howard stepped out of his client meeting, he shot off a curt, though seemingly unrelated, reply to Robert: "I can't believe you left me hanging in our meeting with Jane."

Two little texts – a sentence each – managed to upset a relationship that had been good for years. It took Robert and Howard weeks to be collegial again, and even then they felt the damage linger.

There are so many lessons in this brief but havoc-wreaking exchange. Some are easy: Don't text when you're angry. Ever. In fact, don't communicate in the clutch of any strong negative feeling. Most of us should not use writing to express anger or frustration or disappointment; subtleties of feeling are often lost in texts and e-mails. And, of course, never check your phone in the middle of a meeting.

Being a skillful communicator takes thoughtfulness. So much of our communication has become transactional – a word here, a sentence there – that we forget communication, at its essence, is relational. It's about connection.

It sounds simple, but in reality there is nothing simple about communicating, especially when emotions are involved. I – and you, I am sure – see this kind of clumsy communication all the time. At one point or other we've all been Howard and we've all been Robert. Situations like this should encourage us to step back and commit to a clear, straightforward, easy-to-follow framework for communicating powerfully in any situation.

For starters, always plan your communication. As you do, remember that organizations are complex, people make mistakes, and what looks like political backstabbing may be a simple oversight. In difficult situations it helps to ask instead of demand, to stay curious, and to open up conversation rather than shut it down. Give the other person some benefit of the doubt. Your thoughtfulness conveys trustworthiness.

Here are four questions to ask yourself before communicating.

1. **What outcome do I want?** It seems obvious, but in reality it's unusual that we ask this question. Often we react to what other people are saying, to our own emotions, or to a particular situation. But those reactions lead to haphazard outcomes. Start by thinking about the outcome you're aiming for, and then respond in a way that will achieve that outcome. In Robert and Howard's situation, the outcomes they wanted were very similar: to be connected, to be supported, to be

included. Yet their reactions to each other brought them the exact opposite: disconnection.

2. **What should I communicate to achieve that outcome?**
    Once you know your outcome, identifying what you want to say is much easier. If I want to be closer to someone, "I'm hurt that you didn't include me" is clearly a better choice than "I can't believe you didn't include me!" That small word difference represents a huge shift in meaning. Of course, for many of us it's emotionally much easier to say "I'm angry" than to say "I'm hurt." One feels powerful, the other vulnerable. But I'm hurt is more true, more clear, and therefore, more trustworthy. This is one reason why emotional courage is so critical to being an effective communicator and a powerful leader.

3. **How should I communicate to achieve that outcome?**
    Your goal here should be to increase your chances of being heard. So instead of considering how you can most clearly articulate your point, think about how you can predispose the other person to listen. Ironically, you don't do this by speaking at all. Instead, follow the advice from Chapter 14: Stay Open – How to Really Listen. Be curious and ask questions. Recap what you're hearing. Then, before sharing your perspective, ask if you've understood the other person's. If not, ask what you missed. If you hear a yes, ask, "Can I share my perspective?" A yes to this last question is an agreement to listen. And since you just gave a great example of listening, the other person is far more likely to return the favor.

4. **When should I communicate to achieve that outcome?**
    For many of us, communication is a gut reaction. Robert shot off his text the moment he heard he had been left out. Howard immediately responded with his own text in reaction to Robert's. Neither one of them paused or were thoughtful about when they should communicate. The rule here is simple: Don't communicate just because you feel like it. Communicate when you are most likely to be received well.

Ask yourself when you are most likely to approach the communication with curiosity, compassion, and clarity, and when the other person is likely to be generous and calm.

The problem with most communication is that it's easy. Anyone can thoughtlessly type out a 20-second text or a three-sentence e-mail. But communication is a direct line into a complex web of emotion that explodes easily. Robert and Howard found that out the hard way.

Remember, an explosion can be avoided with a few simple questions that, in most cases, take just seconds to answer. And, in those cases when you slip up and communicate unskillfully, there's actually a very simple, straightforward way out of the jam ...

CHAPTER 23

OWN YOUR STUFF

I WANT YOU TO APOLOGIZE

I was backing out of a space in a mall parking lot in New Jersey when, out of the corner of my eye, I saw movement and instinctively slammed on my brakes. Another car sped by, missing me by inches.

I was instantly furious. I pulled out fast to chase the other car, leaning on my horn and flashing my lights. Finally, the car stopped and I pulled up right behind him, still honking. We both got out of our cars.

"What the hell were you thinking? You almost hit me!" I screamed.

"I didn't see you!" he yelled back.

"Of course you didn't. You were driving way too fast!"

We yelled at each other for a few seconds and then he opened his arms wide and shouted:

"What do you want from me?"

An awkward silence hung between us for a moment. That was actually a great question. What *did* I want from him?

I knew he shouldn't have been driving recklessly and I was angry enough to drive recklessly behind him to tell him. What I really wanted was impossible; I wanted him not to have done what he did. Well, too late.

So what did I want now? Why was I screaming at him? The brief pause calmed us both down a little.

101

"I want you to apologize," I told him.

"I'm sorry," he said.

"Thanks," I said feeling strangely better, and we both got back into our cars and drove off without another word.

We have big problems in this country. I don't remember a time when people were so angry with one another. When politics were so vicious.

But we have one more, deeper problem that's making all these other problems worse.

No one is apologizing. No one is taking responsibility for what they did to contribute to our problems. They're all blaming someone or something else. We have a kindergartener's problem and it's tearing us apart.

A friend of mine, Paul Rosenfield, was skiing with his then six-year-old son Yonah when Yonah fell. It was not a terrible fall, but the binding didn't release and Yonah broke his leg. After an emotionally wrenching day spent in the emergency room tending to his child, Paul went to the shop to return the skis and speak with the owner.

The owner of the shop immediately became defensive. He claimed the bindings were set within the normal acceptable range for Yonah's 40-pound weight (in fact one reading showed the binding set above 60 pounds). He claimed he used a special machine to calibrate the setting, a machine that had been used in several court cases. And he initially resisted Paul's request to see the printout from the machine's test.

Paul went into the shop to have a conversation and he left angry enough to sue.

I asked him what the shop owner could have said that would have given him a different feeling.

"If he had been more concerned with the injury than protecting himself, if he had apologized, if he hadn't tried to cover over the fact that the bindings were too tight, if he hadn't given me a hard time about asking for a copy of the measurement printout, if he hadn't mentioned how many times his machine was used in lawsuits, then I would have left feeling less angry."

We try so hard to protect ourselves from lawsuits that we bring on lawsuits. We forget that we are human beings dealing with other human beings. And what human beings want more than anything is empathy – to be cared for and treated with respect. That's trustworthy.

By avoiding responsibility, empathy, and apology, the shop owner became a target for all of Paul's anger about the accident. He proved himself untrustworthy.

In a study of medical malpractice lawsuits, the top five reasons people gave for initiating the lawsuit were:

1. So that it would not happen to anyone else.
2. I wanted an explanation.
3. I wanted the doctors to realize what they had done.
4. To get an admission of negligence.
5. So that the doctor would know how I felt.

And the number one thing the doctor or hospital could have done to prevent the lawsuit? An explanation and apology.

When the University of Michigan Health System experimented with full disclosure, existing claims and lawsuits dropped from 262 in 2001 to 83 in 2007.

Apologies work. Real, heartfelt empathy between one person and another diffuses anger and builds relationships. It reflects trustworthiness. Defensiveness and resistance to admit mistakes creates anger.

If you don't admit mistakes, you can't apologize for them. And if you don't apologize for them, you will generate anger and fighting.

Apologizing is a humane gesture, a way to treat others with respect. It communicates your care and helps the other person know that you see them. And letting others know that you see them does more to develop connection than almost anything else. It's worth some explicit attention ...

CHAPTER 24

LET OTHERS KNOW YOU SEE THEM

20 SECONDS TO A BETTER BONUS

Larry was a mid- to senior-level employee at Overlook, a technology company. I began to work with him while he was running a project to bring Overlook's newest technology tool to the marketplace. Despite a number of obstacles, some of which came from inside Overlook, Larry delivered the product on time and pretty much on budget. He received a solid bonus that year.

Which is why I was surprised when he told me he was leaving Overlook because of the bonus. It was the last straw, he told me. And it wasn't the size of the bonus that bothered him; he agreed it was reasonable. It was how he received it.

His manager just left the check on his chair without a word. Now you might think that doesn't sound so terrible. Why does Larry care how he received his bonus? He should be happy to have one, especially a good one. Larry must be one complicated, hard-to-please prima donna.

But he's not. More than once Larry was described to me as a boy scout, the kind of guy who would routinely stay late to help colleagues through a tight deadline. He was smart, hardworking, humble, and reliable.

In other words, Larry was the kind of guy Overlook shouldn't want to lose. So what went wrong?

To understand that, we need to understand what a bonus means. On one level, it's simple: a bonus means more money.

But it doesn't take long to get more complicated than that. If I asked you to guess which bonus people would prefer, $50,000 or $100,000, you'd guess $100,000. Pretty obvious, right? But, according to researchers Sara Solnick and David Hemenway, the answer is: It depends.

The researchers asked people if, assuming prices for goods and services remained the same, they would rather earn $50,000 a year while other people made $25,000, or earn $100,000 a year while others made $250,000. About half preferred the $50,000.

That's because a bonus is not just money and the things money can buy. It's feedback. We want to know how we're doing. And one of the clearest ways we get the message is by comparing ourselves to others.

But, for so many reasons, that's a losing game. It's one of the reasons I'm not a fan of ranking employees. Each employee adds value in a distinct way, using his or her unique strengths to address particular problems or opportunities.

A manager's most important job is to match the right person to the right job, which makes it virtually impossible to compare one person to another. That's the advantage – and challenge – of diversity.

So how do you escape the comparison trap? You make sure that each employee doesn't simply understand that you value him but also understands, very specifically, why.

Ultimately each one of us cares about three things:

1. Achieving challenging goals
2. Being loved and appreciated
3. Having power/influence

That's it. Money is simply a symbol, a surrogate, for these three things. If I get paid well, it communicates to me that you appreciate me, I have influence, and I've achieved my goals.

But, it is possible that you can pay someone well without clearly communicating those things. And if that's the case, the money loses its power. This is what happened to Larry.

See, Larry hadn't received any meaningful feedback, praise, or supportive communication during the course of the year. He had very little relationship with his manager and only a vague sense of how he was viewed in the organization. When he found the check sitting on his chair, with not so much as a note of thanks for his hard work and dedication, the absence was louder than the presence. His financial needs were met, but his psychological needs were neglected.

This problem is so prevalent you would think it's hard to solve. But it couldn't be easier.

Larry's manager could have personally handed the check to him and, no matter what the amount, said, "Larry, this is all we could do this year, but I want you to know that it doesn't begin to reflect the contribution you've added to me, our department, and to Overlook. You've spent a year of your life dedicated to making this project successful, sometimes even fighting with me to make it work, and I really appreciate that. You can't put a monetary value on that. Thank you."

That's it. Clear, trustworthy, and less than 20 seconds. (Yeah, I timed it.) That's what it would have taken to keep Larry.

Of course, being trustworthy is all about consistency and Larry isn't dumb; if he heard that speech once a year after being ignored for 12 months, he wouldn't believe it. So the reality is, it takes more than 20 seconds. It would have taken 20 seconds once a week to tell Larry what he did that week that was appreciated. That's about 20 minutes a year. To work it needs to be personal, specific, clear, and heartfelt. And that *would be* trustworthy.

But even once a year is a good start. I know a construction firm that didn't have much money for bonuses one year. So, instead of doling out checks for a few hundred bucks, the COO took all the project managers to a high-end men's store where they were measured for, and then sent, a custom fitted shirt. Cost? $150 per employee. Impact? Their feeling of connection and being appreciated. Value? Priceless.

The COO thought about what they would want. He put effort into it. And by doing that, he communicated that he appreciated them, liked them, and recognized the value they brought to him and the firm. That's more value than a check five times the size.

By the way, the things that work at the office? They work at home too. Don't waste a great present by just giving it. Think about what you want to say and then, well, say it. Let the other person know how much you value her and why. How you appreciate what she's achieved, how she's influenced you, how much you like or love her.

So, you might be wondering, what happened to Overlook? Larry was part of a larger exodus. When senior management was asked about it they answered, "We can always replace people." Which is a good thing, because they had to do it a lot.

ELEMENT THREE

COMMIT TO PURPOSE

Build Your Confidence
- Know Who You Are
- Become Who You Want To Be

Connect with Others
- Be Curious and Trusting
- Be Clear and Trustworthy

Commit to Purpose
- **Energize Your Focus**
- **Focus Their Energy**

Cultivate Emotional Courage
- Feel Courageously
- Act Boldly

You have built your confidence and increased your connection with others. Together, those two elements provide a sturdy platform for enrolling and engaging everyone to work together toward a larger purpose, something bigger than all of you. This is where you use the best of who you are – and the best of everyone else – to make a difference, to create something, to build something, to make something happen. Committing to a larger purpose is critical to great leadership, but it's also critical to simply living a good life. Purpose is where you – and those around you – find meaning.

In Part One of this section, Energize Your Focus, you will ignite – or perhaps reignite – your passion. What's worth throwing all your energy into? What will give you meaning and make the best use of your confidence and your connections to others? The chapters in this part will help you translate your passion into a clear focus and they will help you prioritize that focus – so you communicate with strength and clarity, "move the needle" on what matters most, and identify (and stick to) a process that will channel your energy towards achieving that purpose.

In Part Two of this section, Focus Their Energy, you will learn specific tactics and practical techniques to create accountability and inspire action towards your larger purpose. You will learn why it's so important to involve people early and how to follow up in the right ways to ensure their follow-through and true ownership. The chapters in this part will help you develop the mindset and skills to bring out the absolute best in others, while inspiring their collective, aligned action toward this larger purpose to which you've committed.

PART ONE

ENERGIZE YOUR FOCUS

CHAPTER 25

PLAY HARD

NADAL IS STRONG ENOUGH TO CRY; ARE YOU?

Rafael Nadal, who has won 14 Grand Slams and 69 titles during his career so far, is my hero.

His athleticism is extraordinary. His focus is awe-inspiring. His skill is, clearly, second to none. His will is unremitting. It's a joy to watch him in competition. Yet those are not the reasons he's my hero. In fact, it wasn't until after he won the 2013 US Open that he rose to role model in my book.

So what was it?

Immediately after winning, he fell to the ground, crying, then leapt for joy, then lay back on the tennis court, face down, sobbing. After a few moments, he got up and hugged Novak Djokovic, his opponent.

"Now that," I told Isabelle, who was watching with me, "is what it looks like when you put your whole self into something!"

Where is that energy in our companies today? Where are the people leaping for joy, pumping their fists in the air, or weeping, either with happiness or grief?

I sometimes walk through the halls of various companies, looking at people working numbly at their desks or cubicles or nodding off in meetings, wondering, "where are the *people*?"

I'm not advocating for a workplace of loose cannons. I am advocating for a workplace of passionate, engaged, thrilled human beings, committed to a larger purpose, inspiring action to make our most important work happen.

Before his emotional outburst, Nadal played for hours, channeling the energy coursing through his body with controlled responses and deliberate, calculated movements. In other words, he managed his emotions.

That's appropriate; it's how any of us achieve any challenging objective, and we've become very good at it. It's the ultimate example of energized focus.

But after the game, where does all that energy go? Nadal's post-game response was the natural eruption of energy pent up from the concentration of his game.

That's appropriate too. Yet how many of us unrelentingly repress our emotions, or eat and drink them back down?

Years ago, when emotional intelligence became the next big thing, I thought that, perhaps, it would give us permission to express ourselves more authentically in our workplaces. It might teach us how to hold the emotions of others, to sit quietly, empathically, with someone who was crying, without trying to fix what was wrong. Or to celebrate our successes without losing our compassion toward others, whether they are friends or opponents.

But that never happened. For the most part, emotional intelligence is simply new jargon for discussing our emotions intellectually or codifying them in competency models. Meanwhile our feelings remain imprisoned in our heads.

That's not the world I want to live in, and I don't think you really want to live there either. Sure, it might keep us comfortable. Certainly it might feel safe. But only in the short run. Long term, keeping our emotions nice and presentable hurts us, hurts our relationships, leads to burn out, and makes us sick.

So why don't we all live our lives with Nadal's open passion, with his energized focus, with his exposed heart?

Because you can't energize your focus without being emotionally engaged. And it's scary to be emotionally open. It makes us vulnerable. We may feel shame, and we're likely to feel weak.

When I watched Nadal lying face down on the court, his body heaving with sobs, I was reminded of a time when I did the same, in very different circumstances. Earlier in my career, a colleague of mine was very angry about something I had done. In front of several other people, she proceeded to tell me everything I was doing that was making her angry.

My job, in that situation, was to listen to her without defensiveness. I had a very hard time doing that (I kept trying to interrupt to explain myself), but the people around us helped me; when I tried to talk, they gently reminded me to just listen and, when I did, they told me how much they appreciated it.

As I took in her criticisms, my body began to vibrate and, after a while, visibly shake. I couldn't control it. I can't explain it other than I felt like my body was trying to contain all the energy that was coming at me from her, as well as all the energy brewing inside me. After a while, it was simply too much for me to contain and I just burst into sobs.

I felt exposed and ashamed. Not so much by the way my colleague was attacking me as by my physical reaction. That felt painful.

But I also felt a massive release. I felt unburdened, like there was nothing left for me to hide. I felt completely and fully myself. And that was tremendously pleasurable.

I also felt like I could finally take in what my colleague was saying, without agreeing with everything she said but also without making her wrong or judging her. That felt important.

And what I thought might lead to my rejection led to connection. The people around me supported and comforted me.

My sobbing came from failure, Nadal's came from success. I have experienced both, and here's what's interesting: They feel the same. That's because, essentially, they are. It's all energy looking for a way out.

We are, fundamentally, emotional beings. In celebration or sadness, fear or anger or love, our emotions are very much a part of who we are.

It's high time we openly embrace them.

Your emotions are fuel to energize your focus. They are also signals that point you in the direction of what your most important work might be, what focus you want, or even need, to energize. Clues in your body about what is most important to you. Feel deeply and listen carefully to what your body is telling you – knowing where you're going is essential to getting there ...

CHAPTER 26

KNOW WHERE YOU'RE GOING

DEFINE YOUR BIG ARROW

I was facilitating the two-day executive offsite of a mid-sized technology company. The goal of the meeting was to solve major issues and identify potential opportunities that would guide their efforts, as a company, for the next year.

We were halfway through the first day and, while everything was going according to plan, I couldn't shake this nagging feeling that something wasn't right. I struggled to put my finger on it.

I took in the scene. The CEO and all his direct reports were sitting around the board room table and everyone was engaged. People were being respectful, listening to each other without interrupting, asking clarifying questions, and moving efficiently from one presentation to the next. Everyone seemed satisfied; the presentations and conversations were useful and clear.

Because everyone seemed satisfied, I was hesitant to intervene. Still, something felt off. I walked around the room to try to get different perspectives, to see the meeting through the eyes of each person. Finally, when I got to the CEO, and imagined the meeting from his vantage point, it clicked.

Taken one by one, each presentation was tight, well thought out, and deftly delivered. But if you took a bird's eye view, you'd see utter chaos.

117

Figure 26.1   Arrows of chaos.

Each person, representing a different part of the company, had his or her own priorities, concerns, agenda, and goals that weren't aligned with – or in some cases were directly opposed to – the next person's. No one had the whole company perspective in mind. No one was working within a single, overarching, companywide strategy. No one was reflecting a clear commitment to a larger purpose.

If I were to graphically depict this meeting, with each person's objectives, projects, and priorities symbolized by little arrows, it would look like Figure 26.1.

Each leader was thinking about his or her arrows – their piece of the company – but no one was focused on the company as a whole. Again, no commitment to the larger purpose.

If each leader were running an independent company, it would be fine. But they weren't. A decision in R & D affects engineering, manufacturing, marketing, and sales. And if sales decides to focus on different customers, that affects support as well as marketing and even human resources; who you hire and how you manage and pay them might be different.

Here's the thing: These were all smart, competent, highly educated, experienced leaders. It's not that they didn't understand the importance of a solid unified strategy or the importance of committing to a larger purpose. It's not even that they didn't have one. It's just that, amid all the day-to-day challenges and tempting opportunities, they were neglecting it.

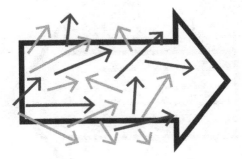

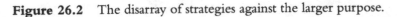

Figure 26.2   The disarray of strategies against the larger purpose.

What they needed was a reminder.

After the next presentation was complete, I asked to pause the meeting and I drew the random set of small arrows on a flip chart. Then I drew a single, big arrow in the middle of them, so the drawing looked like Figure 26.2.

"All these presentations make perfect sense and represent sound strategies if taken independently," I said, "But they're not aligned as an integrated whole with the strategy that we articulated so carefully many months ago."

"I want to remind us of our big arrow: the direction we deliberately chose to move as a company. Our overarching strategy. The big arrow represents where the company is going. It represents the larger purpose that we are all committed to working toward, together. That we're all committed to achieving, together. It contains our priorities, our brand, and the definition of our success. We need to review the decisions we're making from that perspective, so the little arrows align with the big arrow. We need to identify what's distracting and what's strategic."

I started crossing out some arrows and redirecting others. "The implications of this are real; some projects will be stopped, others changed drastically, and some, possibly, shifted a bit."

It got so messy that I just ripped off that page and drew a new, clean image on the flip chart shown in Figure 26.3.

"This is how we should be moving forward as a senior leadership team, together, supporting each other and the larger company,

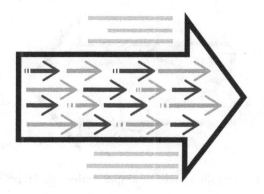

Figure 26.3   Aligning strategies to achieve the shared purpose.

working toward a shared purpose bigger than any one of us or our businesses."

They agreed to review the basic tenets of their strategy. We discussed their brand, the kind of customers they wanted to serve and acquire, the products they were optimally positioned to engineer and manufacture, and the outcomes they wanted to produce over the next year.

The entire conversation took 15 minutes.

It went so quickly because they weren't designing a new strategy, they were just reminding themselves of the well-thought-out strategy they had already developed. They were recommitting to their larger purpose.

Then we got to the most challenging work: making decisions. It's challenging because it demands courageous choices about priorities. Which opportunities are we willing to forgo? Which problems could we not afford to ignore?

They nudged and shifted their little arrows in light of the big arrow. A few projects got canceled as distractions. Some of the conversations were heated and some people got defensive. But the conversation was tremendously productive, always respectful, and clearly focused on the big arrow.

As Lewis Carroll wrote in *Alice in Wonderland*, "If you don't know where you are going, any road will get you there." The challenge for leaders is that, while we often know where we're going, it's easy to get distracted and lose sight of our larger purpose.

Two things are helpful to stay on track:

1. **The big arrow.** Every time you meet to discuss opportunities, address challenges, solve problems, or think through a particular decision, spend a few minutes revisiting the big arrow – your larger purpose – first. Start every strategy meeting recommitting to the larger purpose. Remind yourself of the overarching priorities, direction, and boundaries of the company as a whole.

   The big arrow sets the direction, forms the boundaries, energizes your focus, and answers the critical question: Where should we spend our time? And it serves as a decision making filter to assess the viability and productivity of each decision: Does this solution help us move forward in our collective larger purpose?

2. **Emotional courage.** Making the hard, sometimes painful, decisions required to align your little arrows with the company's big arrow is one of the most important jobs of a leader. It's also the most emotionally challenging. Can you say "no" to that tempting opportunity – you know, the one that your customers will love and will clearly be profitable – if it doesn't align with your big arrow? Can you give up something that's clearly in your best interests – it might even increase your bonus at the end of the year – if it's not in the best interests of the company? (We'll talk a lot more about honing your emotional courage in Element 4).

This is hard, but that's what leadership calls us to do. Energize your focus. Define your Big Arrow. This is what will make everyone – you, your colleagues, and the company as a whole – most successful.

Once you've defined your Big Arrow – your larger purpose – you need to further energize that focus, which happens by choosing where to put your attention (and where not to). I would suggest four areas to focus your attention ...

CHAPTER 27

FOCUS WHERE IT MATTERS

FOUR AREAS TO FOCUS YOUR ATTENTION

It was getting close to lunch time and the people seated around the table – the CEO and seven of his direct reports – were clearly getting antsy. But it wasn't because they were hungry. In fact, they'd been eating snacks all morning, mostly out of boredom.

The COO was at the front of the room, talking through slides projected on a screen. The conversation was primarily one way, with the COO explaining and, when necessary, defending his work.

Finally, when we broke for lunch, the CEO took me aside and told me what we all already knew: "This is a waste of time."

When you bring a senior leadership group together in a room, it's a massive commitment of resources. The hotel and food are the least of it. Even the consultant, if you're using one, is a negligible cost compared to the investment of monopolizing the focus of seven or eight highly compensated, time-starved leaders.

Yet how often do those meetings consist of one presentation after the next, while the executives listen numbly or answer e-mails under the table? How often does the conversation involve everything but the big issues that need executive attention?

With all that brainpower around the table, the focus of a senior meeting needs to be conversation, controversy, even conflict – not updates. Leaders should be engaging and struggling with the organization's most critical and difficult-to-solve issues.

So how do you get there? By creating an environment in which people are real, vulnerable, and brave with each other. An environment in which they can expose their weaknesses, break through silos, and engage one another with challenging questions, thinking, and decisions. *That* is what energizes your focus.

My first rule for these meetings is no slide decks. As soon as someone projects slides onto a screen, the entire focus of the room shifts from each other to a single person (at best) or their smartphones (at worst). Neither is useful.

Once the no-slide-deck rule is established, the team needs to choose where to focus their attention. Which brings me to my second rule. When I run senior leadership meetings, I make sure we focus on four things:

1. **Decisions that move the needle.** Don't waste energy talking about expense reports when you should be talking about mergers and acquisitions or a new business line or a reorganization. Incremental improvements are the purview of lower levels of management. One of my clients, the CEO of a company with revenues of a billion dollars, likes to measure this by the number of zeros involved. Are we talking about a $500,000 decision or a $5,000,000 decision? If there aren't enough zeros, the decision isn't strategic enough and shouldn't absorb senior leadership time. Senior leadership should be focused on fundamentals, not incrementals.

2. **The big arrow.** We talked about this in the previous chapter. Think of your company as one big arrow that contains lots of little arrows – projects, businesses, clients, business deals. The big arrow is your larger purpose. If you want to get more laser focused, answer this question: What is the most important outcome to achieve over the next 12 months? The CEO and his or her leadership team own that big arrow. The problem

is that, as we discussed in the last chapter, the little arrows point in different directions as people solidify their silos, bicker amongst themselves, and neglect the larger mission, whether it's intentional or not. Senior leaders have the responsibility to make decisions and act in ways that break through silos and align everyone with the strategic and cultural direction of the company. That's how they can ensure all the arrows will be shooting in the same direction.

3. **The next level of leadership.** One of the most important roles of the most senior leaders is to engage the up-and-coming leaders, fostering their leadership and decision-making. That's how a company grows. Talking about the next level of leadership, developing succession plans, pushing decisions to that level, including them in strategic discussions — those efforts are high return.

4. **Undiscussables.** This one takes the most emotional courage. Talking about the thing that no one is talking about is an almost foolproof way to improve company performance. Maybe it concerns another leader or maybe it has to do with the performance of a certain division. Maybe it's about the CEO's leadership style or a lack of trust among the senior team. Whatever it is, the mere fact that it's important and not being discussed is a solid indication that it's holding the organization back.

Dealing with whatever comes across your desk leaves the control in other people's hands. CEOs and other senior leaders can't afford to be that passive. Every single thing you do as a leader needs to have an impact. Your job is to think big. If the topic is outside the rubric of these four things, then it should be dealt with at a more junior level of the organization.

During lunch, I shared these four points of focus with the CEO and we agreed that the most critical one, for his team, was the way his direct reports were working together. Or rather weren't working together. That had been an undiscussable for some time.

By the time the team got back to the room, the slide projector was gone. At first, people were off-balance. What about the work they had put into their presentations? What about the safety they felt hiding behind slides?

"Your brains are too valuable to sit through presentations," the CEO said, "Your brains need to think together."

Then he threw a zinger on the table: "Look around the room. Who's not getting along with each other? Let's talk about that!"

Silence ensued.

To the CEO's credit, he did nothing to dispel the awkwardness. He tossed the ball and it was their turn to step up and run with it.

Finally, after what felt like forever, one of his direct reports spoke up, admitting what everyone else in the room already knew but never talked about: He and another person in the room were having a hard time working together.

And for the next three hours of lively, engaged, sometimes difficult conversation, not a single person looked at an e-mail under the table.

That's what an energized, focused team looks like. Equally important is energizing your day-to-day focus to drive attention toward your larger purpose (and not everywhere else). That's when you'll want a filter. And there's no better time to use it than on your first day back from vacation . . .

CHAPTER 28

USE YOUR FOCUS AS A FILTER

USE YOUR FIRST DAY BACK FROM VACATION TO ENERGIZE YOUR FOCUS

You come back from vacation and start your game of catch-up. This is an especially challenging game if you're a senior leader. You have hundreds, maybe thousands of e-mails, a backlog of voicemails, and a to-do list that doubled or tripled in length while you were away. You need to respond to the pent-up needs of clients, managers, colleagues, employees, and vendors. You need to fight fires. You need to regain control.

So you do your best to work through the pileup, handling the most urgent items first, and within a few days, you're caught up and ready to move forward. You're back in control. You've won.

Or have you?

If that's your process, you've missed a huge energize-your-focus opportunity.

What's the most important role of a leader? As we already discussed in the past few chapters, it's focus.

As a senior leader, the most valuable thing you can do is to align people behind your business's big arrow and commit to the larger purpose toward which you are all working. If you do that well, the organization will function at peak productivity and have the greatest possible impact. But that's not easy to do. It's hard enough for any one of us to be focused and aligned with our most important objectives. To get an entire organization aligned is crazy hard.

Once in a while, though, you get the perfect opportunity. A time when it's a little easier, when people are more open, when you can be clearer, when your message will be particularly effective.

Coming back from vacation is one of those opportunities. You've gotten some space from the day to day. People haven't heard from you in a while. Maybe they've been on vacation too. They're waiting. They're more influenceable than usual.

Don't squander this opportunity by trying to efficiently wrangle your own inbox and to-do list. Before responding to a single e-mail, consider a few questions:

What's your top imperative for the organization right now? What will make the most difference to the company's results? What behaviors do you need to encourage if you are going to achieve your big arrow? And, perhaps most important, what's less important? Answering these questions will energize your focus.

The goal in answering these questions is to choose three to five major things that will make the biggest difference to the organization. Once you've identified those things, you should spend 95% of your energy moving them forward.

How should you do it?

1. Be very clear about your three to five things. Write them down and choose your words carefully. Read them aloud. Do you feel articulate? Succinct? Clear? Useful? Will they be helpful guides for people when they're making decisions and taking actions? Do they clearly reflect your focus?

2. Use them as the lens through which you look at and filter every decision, conversation, request, to-do, and e-mail you work through. When others make a request, or ask you to make a decision, say to them out loud, "Given that our big arrow is X, then it would make sense to do Y."

Will that e-mail you're about to respond to reinforce your three to five priorities? Will it create momentum in the right direction? If so, respond in a way that tightens the alignment and clarifies the focus by tying your response as closely as you can to one or more of the three to five things, as you have written them.

If you look at an e-mail and can't find a clear way to connect it to the organization's top three to five priorities, then move on to the next e-mail. Don't be afraid to deprioritize issues that don't relate to your top three to five things. This is all about energized focus, and in order to energize your focus on some things, you need to ignore others.

You've got this wonderful opportunity, a rare moment in time when your primary role and hardest task – to focus the organization – becomes a little easier. Don't lose it.

Coming back from vacation isn't simply about catching up. It's about getting ahead. Clarifying your focus and using it as a filter is a critical step. The next step is to build the momentum. That requires repetition ...

CHAPTER 29

You Can't Say It Enough

The Mouthwash Principle: For Energized Focus, Rinse and Repeat

I had what I considered a pretty solid dental routine: Floss and brush twice a day. That's enough, right?

Not according to my new dentist. After hmmming and oooooing and picking and sticking at my teeth, he gave me a new, more cumbersome routine. Now, I floss, then brush, then use a pick between my teeth and, finally, use fluoride and antibacterial washes.

Here's the amazing thing: Often, it's not until the antibacterial wash step that I get every last food particle out. In other words, even all the flossing and the brushing and the picking don't quite get the job done. It takes all that, plus the final swishing, to get everything clean.

I was brushing my teeth this morning, thinking about this as I listened to my local National Public Radio's spring campaign to raise funds. For close to a week now they've been asking for pledges. Each time I heard their request, I decided I would pledge. And yet, I'm embarrassed to say, it took until today – the last day of their pledge drive – to actually donate.

It's the mouthwash principle. And it's critical to powerful leadership. If you want to make an impact on people, to influence their behavior in some way, you have to keep sharing the message, coming at it from different angles and at different times long after you think you're done.

Politicians know this as they give their stump speeches for the thousandth time. So do advertisers, who keep repeating the same jingle over and over again until it sticks in your head.

This may sound obvious, but it's not what most of us do. Many managers and leaders say something once, twice, maybe three times, and expect the message to get through. Then they get exasperated when other people's behavior deviates from the expectations that were so clearly stated.

Here's the problem: There's a big difference between saying something and hearing it.

When you say something, it's probably been brewing for some time. You've already tossed it around in your head, maybe talked to a few other people about it, and then come to a final decision or thought. In other words, you had a process. Plus, you're the one who is saying it so it's probably more important to you than anyone else. Saying it once seems plenty.

But when you hear it or read it, you're doing so for the first time and in the context of many other messages that are flying at you. It's not your message. For the message to rise above the cacophony of other messages and thoughts, it needs to be repeated.

So even though repeating it several times seems excessive to you when you're speaking, it's barely enough to get the message across. It's the mouthwash principle.

Richard, one of my clients, the CEO of a $900 million company, recently used the mouthwash principle well. We were preparing for an offsite and he sent out an email detailing several issues that were up for discussion. There was one thing, however, that the CEO knew would consume too much time in the meeting – we'll call it option D – and it was not up for discussion, even though some people on the team would have liked it to be. So, in the e-mail, he made the point that option D was not up for discussion *three times* – at the beginning, in the middle, and at the end. The last time he wrote it, HE PUT IT IN CAPS.

Then, when he was opening the meeting, after talking about what we would be discussing, he reminded everyone that he knew he was being overbearing about this but he really didn't want to waste time discussing option D. It's the mouthwash principle, and it worked.

This isn't just about impacting others, it also about impacting ourselves. How often have you read something a second time and found things you missed the first? And how often have you thought you learned something, changed a behavior, or made a decision, only to find yourself backsliding? It's why, even though that last book on leadership or communication or time management was really good, you'll probably need to read another one on the same topic soon. It's not that each book doesn't have the perfect formula to make you a flawless leader or communicator or time manager. It's just that you need to go over the same things multiple times in order to get those last specks of counterproductive behavior out of your system.

In other words, even when we're speaking to ourselves, we don't listen that well. Repetition is necessary to energize your own focus.

It's always a good idea to become a better listener. But don't rely on other people's listening as a strategy to solidify your point. What's a better strategy? Become comfortable with repetition. Say things more often than you think necessary and resist the urge to throw your hands up in exasperation when people don't do what you so clearly explained they should. Expect them not to.

This morning, after brushing, flossing, picking, and swishing my own teeth, I asked my kids – for the fourth time – whether they had brushed their teeth. Two out of the three had.

I'm glad I asked that fourth time.

The power of repetition is strong, especially when you are trying to establish and reinforce a single, critical focus. Counterintuitively, the opposite works as well. Sometimes, the power of silence can be just the thing to get others to listen ...

CHAPTER 30

AND SOMETIMES IT'S BETTER TO SAY LESS

IF YOU WANT PEOPLE TO LISTEN, STOP TALKING

George, a managing director at a large financial services firm, had an uncanny ability to move a roomful of people to his perspective. What George said was not always popular, but he was a master persuader.

It wasn't his title – he often swayed colleagues at the same hierarchical level. And it wasn't their weakness – he worked with a highly competitive bunch. It wasn't even his elegant and distinguished British accent – his British colleagues were persuaded right along with everyone else, and none of them had his track record of persuasion.

George had a different edge, which wasn't immediately obvious to me because I was listening to what George said. His power was in what he didn't say.

George was silent more than anyone else who spoke, and often, he spoke last.

I say "anyone else who spoke" because there are plenty of people who remain completely silent – they don't say anything, ever – and they are not persuasive. For many people, silence equals absence. But George was not absently or passively silent. In fact, he was busier in his silence than anyone else was while speaking. He was listening.

It's counterintuitive, but it turns out that listening can be far more persuasive than speaking.

It is easy to fall into the habit of persuasion by argument. But arguing does not change minds – if anything, it makes people more intransigent. Silence is a greatly underestimated source of power. In silence, we can hear not only what is being said but also what is not being said. In silence, it can be easier to reach the truth.

There is almost always more substance below the surface of what people say than there is in their words. They have issues they are not willing to reveal. Agendas they won't share. Opinions too unacceptable to make public.

We can hear all those things – and more – when we keep quiet. We can feel the substance behind the noise.

I could tell what George was doing, because when he decided to speak, he was able to articulate each person's position. And, when he spoke about what they said, he looked at them in acknowledgment, and he linked what they had said to the big arrow, the larger purpose they were pursuing.

Here's what's interesting: Because it was clear that George had heard them, people did not argue with him. And, because he had heard them, his perspective was the wisest in the room.

This relates to another thing George consistently did that made him trustworthy and persuasive. He was always willing to learn something from others' perspectives and to let them know when he was shifting his view as a result of theirs. Incorporating their views served to further energize his focus.

Because words can so often get in the way, silence can help you make connections. Try just listening, for once. It softens everyone, and makes you more willing not only to keep listening, but to incorporate others' perspectives.

If you treat this silence thing as a game, or as a way to manipulate the views of others, it will backfire. Inevitably you will be discovered, and your betrayal will be felt more deeply. If people are lured into connection, only to feel manipulated, they may never trust you again.

You have to use silence with respect.

There are so many good reasons to be thoughtfully silent that it's a wonder we don't do it more often. We don't because it's uncomfortable. It requires that we listen to perspectives with which we may disagree and listen to people we may not like.

But that's what teamwork – and leadership – calls us to do: To listen to others, to see them fully, and to help them connect their desires, perspectives, and interests with the larger purpose that everyone, ultimately, wants to achieve.

There's something else we offer, as persuasive leaders, when we are silent: space for others to step into. Lao Tzu, the ancient Chinese philosopher, wrote: "A leader is best when people barely know he exists, when his work is done, his aim fulfilled, they will say: We did it ourselves."

When people contribute their own ideas, they inevitably work harder than if they are simply complying with our ideas. Silence, followed by a few well-chosen words, is our best bet at achieving this leadership ideal.

So, how do we do it, in practice? We all know how to be silent. The question is: Can we withstand the pressure to speak? That's where emotional courage comes in.

Few resist the urge to speak, which is why we seldom have silent moments in groups. But that, according to George, can be used to our advantage.

"When you ask a question into a group," he told me, "think of it as a competition. If you answer your own question, you've lost. You'll be answering your own questions all day and no one else will do the work. But wait in the silence – no matter how long – until someone in the group speaks. And they will then continue to do the work necessary to lead themselves."

There it is, his secret: Let other people speak into the silence and listen quietly for the truth behind their words. Then acknowledge what you've heard (which is, most likely, more than has been said) and, once the others feel seen and heard, offer your view.

And when they all agree with you? That's the power of silence.

PART TWO

FOCUS THEIR ENERGY

CHAPTER 31

GIFTED, GAME, AND GENEROUS

THREE QUALITIES ALL LEADERS NEED TO CULTIVATE WITHIN THEIR TEAMS

"I want your help developing my direct reports into stronger leaders," John the new CEO of Fasseni, a $350 million technology company, told me several years ago.

Initially, I approached the request like any consultant might.

First, I asked John why he wanted my help. He told me that Fasseni had stagnated. They had been hovering around the same revenue point for years and their competitors were gaining market share. He saw opportunity and knew that success lay in the hands of his direct reports. That made sense to me.

So John and I defined a list of qualities a great leader should have, like expertise in their field, strategic thinking capability, common sense intelligence, powerful communication skills, problem-solving prowess, and similar traits.

Then I spent some time interviewing him and his direct reports to better understand their strengths and weaknesses as they related to the list of leadership qualities we had defined.

Identify the goal, assess the current situation, understand the gap, and then close it. Consulting 101. Simple, right?

Only in this case, it wasn't so simple – because there was no gap.

On the whole, the leaders at Fasseni were smart, capable, communicative, strategic people. A few were even charismatic. They were good leaders. Maybe we could have made incremental improvements, but, I told John, I didn't believe it would be a good use of his resources. Our work wouldn't move the needle enough.

We sat in silence for a moment and then I chanced a gut feeling. "There is one more thing I'd love to do. I can't exactly tell you why, but I'd love to see your direct reports in a meeting together." He hesitated – so far I hadn't added much value – but he took a risk.

Here's what I saw:

One item on the agenda was the slowdown in sales. When that conversation started, the head of sales started to defend his organization. Prices are too high, he said, because of the CEO's focus on margins. If manufacturing could reduce costs, then sales would pick up.

Hold on, the head of manufacturing argued, we can't reduce costs because of the way the product is engineered. If engineering didn't overcomplicate things, the product would be cheaper to build.

Wait a second, retorted the head of engineering, we're only responding to what marketing is telling us we have to create to meet customer demand. If we didn't have to be so customized for each unique customer situation, we could engineer a more efficient product.

And so the conversation continued, like a game of hot potato, everyone hoping, desperately, that the blame wouldn't land with him when the song ended.

"We've been focused on the wrong problem," I told John at dinner that night. "You asked me to help you develop your direct reports into strong leaders. But they're already strong leaders … individually. They're just not strong leaders *collectively*."

Each leader ran his organization successfully, aggressively pursuing his organization's interests. And each one succeeded in meeting – often exceeding – his goals. Each one was committed to – and cared deeply about – his organization's performance.

But that's all they cared about – their own organizations. They were impressive as leaders, but destructive as a leadership team. Similar to what I described in Chapter 26 (Know Where You're Going – Define Your Big Arrow), their arrows were going in very independent, chaotic directions. In that chapter, I talked about what they needed to do collectively as a team to identify their big arrow and align their individual arrows.

Here I'm asking a different question: What kind of *people* do they need to be in order to do that successfully?

In other words, if you are going to successfully focus the energy of the team, who do you want on the team? To be a valued contributor to a larger purpose you need to be three things:

1. **Gifted.** Simply put, leaders need to be good at what they do. Smart, prepared, and well-informed, they need to engage in conversations with curiosity and capability. But to be on a team, they need to go beyond that. They need to be gifted communicators and gifted learners, mastering conflict without being offensive, and adapting to their own changing roles as the organization grows.

2. **Game.** They need to have the courage to take risks. To be vulnerable and open to challenge and criticism, they need to be willing to consider anything. This requires a tremendous amount of confidence. The kind of confidence that allows them to be questioned by others – even take blame and feel threatened – without becoming defensive.

3. **Generous.** They need to put the good of the company above their own department, team, or agenda. They must be good-hearted, mutually respectful, and gracious, resisting the urge to dominate, take the upper hand, or shine at the expense of others. Part of being generous with others also means taking an interest in, learning about, and offering opinions regarding the other team members' functions.

Being gifted, game, and generous is tremendously hard to do because those qualities can make us feel tremendously vulnerable. That's why we need emotional courage. We need that courage if we're going to lead with others and focus the energy of our teams.

John and I started to develop each member of the team – and shape the dynamics of their collaboration – to focus their energy toward these qualities. It took time, hard work, and commitment and it didn't work for everyone. Those who could not bring themselves to be gifted, game, and generous did not remain on the team.

Over time, focusing the energy of the leadership team paid off. Since we started working together, Fasseni has grown from approximately $350 million in revenue to about $1 billion. During that time, the stock price went from around $19 per share to $107.50 per share.

That kind of growth is inevitably driven by a number of factors. But one factor stood out, a single element that gave them a clear advantage compared to their competitors: A gifted, game, and generous leadership team.

Once you have the right team of gifted, game, and generous people, you know the team has the *capacity* to achieve the big arrow. Now you need to help them own it. That's where the farm-to-table secret to focus their energy comes in ...

CHAPTER 32

ENGAGE FROM THE BEGINNING

THE FARM-TO-TABLE METHOD OF FOCUSING THE ENERGY OF YOUR TEAM

The kitchen was a complete mess. I tried to clean the utensils and machines right after I used them but I couldn't keep up with my own cooking frenzy.

I baked one loaf of carrot nut bread and two loaves of zucchini spice bread. I made a carrot-dill soup, a chilled yogurt-cucumber-dill soup, and a kale-swiss chard-carrot soup. I also shredded a beet-mint salad, cooked an eggplant-green pepper-tomato thing, and grilled peppers in the oven.

Just for the record, usually the only thing I ever bake is cookies, by squeezing batter from a store bought tube. If I make dinner, it consists of steamed veggies, rice, and – my pièce de résistance for the kids – frozen pizza. Warmed, of course.

So what possessed me? Why did I work so hard to create such a feast?

My family had spent the weekend at a 10-acre farm.

Our kids had never stayed on a working farm before and were excited. So when they woke up at six in the morning and asked to go see the goats, we went.

Now I don't know if you've ever milked a goat before, but if not, I suggest you find yourself a farm and try it. Not just because it's a cool feeling. Not just because it's good to know how the whole get-milk-from-an-animal thing works. And not because you better know how because one day you might be thirsty and really need to get milk from an animal. It's not a knowledge or understanding or capability thing.

It's an experience thing. Because once you've milked a goat, you'll never drink milk or eat cheese the same way again. You'll choose your milk more carefully. You'll want to know who milked the animal, how that person treated her, and what she ate. And when you drink the milk, you'll have a much deeper appreciation for the taste.

In short, you'll care more about your milk than you ever did before.

After the goats, we went to the vegetable fields where the kids (I include myself here) went crazy. We pulled carrots out of the ground. We broke off stalks of kale and Swiss chard. We gathered bunches of dill. We picked zucchini. We plucked tomatoes. We collected green peppers.

So we returned home with a car filled with fresh produce. And I spent the next day inspired – chopping, shredding, boiling, and baking – preparing more food than I had in months. I needed no external motivation. I had no sense of urgency because guests were coming (they weren't). I had no desire to perform for money (I wasn't making any). There was no need for a proverbial carrot or stick. My motivation came from a real carrot – one I pulled from the ground myself.

Where and when you enter a process is a strong determinant of how connected you'll feel to the outcome. If I'm on the receiving end of a new initiative, I'll approach it more critically than if I'm one of the people involved from the beginning.

New sales process? Don't figure it all out yourself and then tell your sales people about it. Let them figure it out with you. If they do the seeding and weeding and picking, they'll be far more likely to eat the produce. Involve them in the development of the big arrow and their energy will be far more focused on achieving it.

Want customers to buy your service or product? Involve them in the creation of it. The projects I win – and the only ones I do now – are the ones I design with my clients. Those designs are always far better than anything I could propose on my own because they are informed by my clients' deep knowledge of their companies – their culture, personality, and capacity to absorb change. Most important, those projects sell – and succeed – because the people impacted by the work have focused their energy from the get-go on the impact they want to have.

And they're always happier with the outcome. They feel something deeper than the success of a project gone well. They feel pride of ownership. They feel satisfied by the journey that brought them to their success. They feel the confidence that they made it happen and they can do it again.

Ownership goes a long way to inspiring action about what's most important. Once you have ownership, you need to help people follow through on your expectations and their own excitement...

CHAPTER 33

HELPING OTHERS BE TRUSTWORTHY

THE SECRET TO ENSURING FOLLOW-THROUGH

"Listen, I would love the reorg to work. But I just can't trust them."

I had called Elizabeth as part of my preparation for an offsite with the leaders of a fast-growing financial services firm. Elizabeth was talking about the newly reorganized HR department.

Before, when she could trust them, Elizabeth had a dedicated HR person – Lucinda – to address her needs. But now? Now she had to call a shared services group who were, collectively, responsible for following through on her requests.

"Why can't you trust them?" I asked.

Elizabeth had a hard time answering. It wasn't that they had failed to deliver – but she was pretty sure they would. With so many different people involved, how could things not fall through the cracks?

"The more people juggling," Elizabeth told me, "the higher the risk of someone, somewhere, dropping a ball."

True. But there's another, more positive, side to group juggling: The more people juggling, the more likely someone, somewhere, will be able to catch a ball that an otherwise busy, overwhelmed individual would have dropped.

"How do we keep them accountable?" Elizabeth asked, still uncomfortable. "At least with Lucinda, responsibility was clear."

Elizabeth had a point. Which got me thinking: When does a ball usually get dropped? I thought of all the mishaps, mishandles, and mistakes I had witnessed in the past month and realized they could all be traced to a single point in time: the handoff.

For the most part, problems didn't arise because of incompetence, laziness, or disinterest. They arose because of poor communication. At the moment two people were discussing what needed to get done, something, somehow, went awry.

The solution can't be as simple as one point of contact because, in a large, complex, global organization, one point of contact is never simple. The solution has to be even simpler than that. It has to work with one point of contact or many. It has to work across the hierarchy, across departments, and across all silos.

As I finished my pre-offsite interviews, I made a single request of each leader: Read *The Checklist Manifesto* by Atul Gawande.

A physician and writer, Gawande describes doctors who resist the checklist – it's too simple, insulting even – and then shows us how hospital staff who follow checklists save more lives than most medical "miracle drugs" or procedures.

Gawande makes a strong case for why experts need checklists, especially for the most mundane of tasks. The more expert we are in something, the more we take things for granted, and, as a result, miss the obvious.

Most of us think we communicate well, which, ironically, is why we often leave out important information (we believe others already know it). Or we fail to be specific about something (we think others already understand it). Or we resist clarifying (we don't want to insult other people).

Thankfully, there's a simple solution: Create a checklist and use it during every handoff.

During the offsite, the leadership team looked at where problems happened in the past and where they were likely to happen in the future. Almost all were during handoffs.

So we developed the following mandatory "handoff check-list" – questions that the person handing off work must ask the person taking accountability for delivery:

HANDOFF CHECKLIST

1. What do you understand the priorities to be?
2. What concerns or ideas do you have that have not already been mentioned?
3. What are your key next steps, and by when do you plan to accomplish them?
4. What do you need from me in order to be successful?
5. Are there any key contingencies we should plan for now?
6. When will we next check-in on progress/issues?
7. Who else needs to know our plans, and how will we communicate them?

Time it takes to go through the checklist? One to five minutes. Time (and trust) saved by going through the checklist? Immeasurable.

We came up with this checklist because it addressed the most common reasons for dropping balls in this particular organization. Your handoff checklist may be different. Just make sure it's standard operating procedure for everyone. When you go through the checklist and answer the questions, you'll be able to quickly identify any misunderstandings and correct them on the spot, saving weeks of misdirected work and the loss of trust that goes along with it.

Meanwhile, you get real time visibility on – and leverage to re-focus – where they're about to spend their energy. That's the power of the checklist.

A few months after the offsite, I called Elizabeth to ask her how it was working. Was the new HR Shared Services organization delivering? Did she miss Lucinda?

"Sure I miss Lucinda," she told me, "but I don't need her."

Then she pulled out her checklist to make sure we were both on the same page for our work going forward.

Checklists are an ideal way to ensure crystal clarity on what's expected. The next step is holding people accountable for execution...

CHAPTER 34

CREATING ACCOUNTABILITY

FIVE BUILDING BLOCKS FOR A CULTURE OF ACCOUNTABILITY

John was doing his best to be calm, but his frustration was palpable. Jeanine was explaining that there was little chance her group was going to make the numbers for this quarter. "Honestly?" she said. "The numbers weren't realistic to begin with. It was really unlikely that we were going to make them."

That's when John lost it. "You agreed to the numbers in our budget meeting! You came up with them!"

Jeanine was silent for a while. Then she stammered out a weak defense that John promptly tore apart. Later, when John and I were debriefing the conversation, he asked me a question that I have heard countless times from countless leaders.

"How do I get my people to be more accountable for results?"

Accountability is not simply taking the blame when something goes wrong. It's not a confession. Accountability is about delivering on a commitment. It's ensuring that your team's energy is focused on taking responsibility for targeting the big arrow, the larger purpose, not just a set of tasks. It's taking initiative with thoughtful, strategic follow-through.

And it's necessary at all levels of the hierarchy. Executives high on the org chart can't really be accountable unless the people who report

153

to them also follow through on their commitments. This is a struggle, of course. I have seen leaders direct, question, and plead. I have seen them yell, act passive-aggressively, and throw up their hands in frustration – all in the service of "holding people accountable."

None of that works. Getting angry with people when they fall short is not a productive process for holding people accountable. It almost always reduces motivation and performance.

So what can we do to focus energy by creating accountability in the people around us? We need to aim for clarity in five areas (Remember the checklists we talked about in the last chapter? Think of this as your accountability checklist):

1. **Clear expectations.** The first step is to be crystal clear about what you expect. This means being clear about the outcome you're looking for, how you'll measure success, and how people should go about achieving the objective. It doesn't all have to come from you. In fact, the more skilled your people are, the more ideas and strategies should be coming from them. Have a genuinely two-way conversation, and before it's over, ask the other person to summarize the important pieces – the outcome they're going for, how they are going to achieve it, and how they'll know whether they're successful – to make sure you're ending up on the same page. Writing out a summary is a good idea but doesn't replace saying it out loud.

2. **Clear capability.** What skills does the person need to meet the expectations? What resources will they need? If the person does not have what's necessary, can they acquire what's missing? If so, what's the plan? If not, you'll need to delegate to someone else. Otherwise you're setting them up for failure.

3. **Clear measurement.** Nothing frustrates leaders more than being surprised by failure. Sometimes this surprise is because the person who should be delivering is afraid to ask for help. Sometimes it comes from premature optimism on both sides.

Either way, it's completely avoidable. During the expectations conversation, you should agree on weekly milestones with clear, measurable, objective targets. If any of these targets slip, jump on it immediately. Brainstorm a solution, identify a fix, redesign the schedule, or respond in some other way that gets the person back on track.

4. **Clear feedback.** Honest, open, ongoing feedback is critical. People should know where they stand. If you have clear expectations, capability, and measurement, the feedback can be fact-based and easy to deliver. Is the person delivering on her commitments? Is she working well with the other stakeholders? If she needs to increase her capability, is she on track? The feedback can also go both ways — is there something you can be doing to be more helpful? Give feedback weekly, and remember: it's more important to be helpful than nice.

5. **Clear consequences.** If you've been clear in all of the ways already mentioned, you can be reasonably sure that you did what's necessary to support their performance. At this point, you have three choices: repeat, reward, or release. Repeat the preceding steps if you feel that there is still a lack of clarity in the system. If the person succeeded, you should reward them appropriately (acknowledgement, promotion, etc.). If they have not proven accountable and you are reasonably certain that you followed the steps, then they are not a good fit for the role, and you should release them from it (change roles, fire them, etc.).

These are the building blocks for a culture of accountability. The magic is in the way they work together as a system. If you miss any one, accountability will fall through that gap.

I've found that it's useful to make this list public and to discuss it with the people you're asking to be accountable before there's a specific project on the line.

When I explained all of this to John, it was easy for him to identify the gaps in his communication with Jeanine. His expectations were clear, but her capability was lacking, which they had never addressed. This is where energy was being drained out of the system. Once they'd spoken about the gap, he could support her development with coaching while also reviewing her milestones more frequently. That gave him the data he needed to give her clear and timely feedback. With that kind of clarity and communication, the energy leak was plugged and Jeanine got traction on her key contributions to the big arrow.

Remember the question we started with, the one that plagues so many leaders: "How do I get my people to be more accountable for results?"

Now there's an answer: It depends. Which of the five areas have you neglected?

Once you know you have a strong team, you've focused their energy on the larger purpose, and you've set up the structures and practices to ensure follow-through and accountability, it's time to let them loose ...

CHAPTER 35

BIGGER THAN YOU

WHY LEADERS SHOULD TRY TO BE OVERWHELMED

This was the fourth day of our five days together, and we were swirling in chaos. There were almost 30 of us in a small room as part of Ann Bradney's leadership workshop I wrote about earlier in this book.

Sara was on the floor, cradling the arm and leg she had broken several months earlier, feeling broken herself, crying as she thought about her son who died five years ago. A few feet away from her, Angelo stood with his hands on his chest, also crying, immersed in his experience of alienation from his mother. Across the room, Zoe was huddled with her sister, Chloe, as they felt the pain of losing their own mother and confronted their fear of losing each other.

As I looked around the room, I saw two or three other people scattered about, each struggling with deep emotions of loss, fear, anger, and sadness. The noise was disorienting. People were crying, laughing, shouting, hugging, and comforting each other, all at the same time. It was completely out of control.

Just like life itself.

We were a microcosm of the world and of every organization I've ever known. Not just the pain, though that certainly exists wherever we're brave enough to look, but the multiplicity of activity. The variety of individuals and groups, each occupied, engulfed even, by their own concerns, needs, and desires.

To top it off, we had only one established leader, Ann, to manage the mayhem. It was an impossible job. She couldn't be in seven places at once. She couldn't support each of the people who needed her. She had set herself up to fail.

It eventually dawned on me that was her plan all along.

Ann didn't just let the chaos happen by accident. She encouraged it. Because the perfect ingredient to draw out leadership is exactly the one most of us, including leaders, fight so hard to avoid: being overwhelmed.

Leaders like to be in control. I know that's true for me. I want things to turn out right and I feel – often mistakenly – that if I have control over them, they will.

But here's the thing: The more control I have over something, the less room there is for other people to step into their own leadership. If Ann didn't need the help, many of us would have sat back watching, happy to let her lead.

When I took a bird's-eye view of the room, I saw that there were only six, maybe seven, people who needed help at that moment. The rest of us, close to 20, were in physical, psychological, and emotional places where we could offer help.

But it's hard to offer help, to step into your own leadership. It requires tremendous courage. You have to risk being wrong, over-stepping your bounds, and standing alone.

That's why we needed a nudge.

So Ann created a situation that she couldn't possibly handle by herself, and people stepped up. One participant, Janice, went over to Zoe and Chloe, the two sisters, and spoke softly to them. Another partici-pant, Holly, sat next to Sara, the woman mourning the loss of her son, and held her. And I went over to Angelo, who looked up at me for a moment and then fell into my arms crying.

It's not that Janice, Holly, and I were the leaders in the workshop. The day before, it was me who was crying, and Angelo who did the comforting. But on this day, in this moment, we were in a position to reach out.

Designing chaos into a process is the antithesis of what most leaders do. Usually, we try to focus on one thing at a time: one objective, one concept, one conversation, one task.

But in real life, in real organizations, nothing happens one thing at a time. And no one can be on top of it all. At one point, one of the participants accused Ann of allowing too much bedlam. Ann's response was swift and emphatic:

"No. People want to make the leader the one who sees and knows everything. I am just a human being. I can't see everything. I can't know everything. I make mistakes. When you make me more than human, you can bring me down while refusing to take responsibility or any risk. Step into your leadership now."

In other words, she told the group that, at this point, we were capable of taking everything we knew, all our ownership and skill and focus on the larger purpose, and running with it ourselves.

But wait a second. It sounds great but what if everyone in an organization stepped into his or her own leadership? What if everyone followed his or her own impulse? Wouldn't that lead to anarchy?

Maybe. It depends on the strength of their organization's container. How clear is the big arrow, the larger purpose? How clear is the vision? The values? The culture? If we know what we're doing, why we're doing it, what's important to us, and how we operate, then there will be trust, focused energy, and abundant, unified leadership. If not, there will be anarchy.

But if the container isn't strong, if people are not unified around a larger purpose, there will be anarchy anyway. Because, no matter how much leaders would like to, they just can't control everything. And trying to control the uncontrollable just makes things worse. People check out. They feel no ownership. They work the minimum. And things fall through the cracks.

Once you've done everything we've been talking about in the book so far – standing in your confidence, connected with others, committed to a larger purpose, you are ready to let go. That's the highest level of focusing their energy – letting them do it themselves.

Here's the hard part: leading without controlling. Stepping into your own leadership while leaving space for others to step into theirs as well. The more people are engaged, the more they will rally their energy in support of your shared purpose.

When you do let go, there's an inevitable side effect: People will make mistakes. And how you respond to their mistakes, failures, or struggles will either reinforce their losing streak or reenergize and inspire them to succeed ...

CHAPTER 36

IMPROVING PERFORMANCE AFTER A CRITICAL ERROR (PACE)

HOW TO REACT WHEN SOMEONE DISAPPOINTS

"Why?" the CEO of the hedge fund yelled at one of his portfolio managers. "Why would you increase that investment? What were you thinking?"

The portfolio manager muttered a weak defense, which the CEO promptly tore to shreds.

When the manager left his office, the CEO turned to me, exasperated. "How do you reverse a losing streak?" he asked.

"Not like that," I said.

High performing leaders expect a lot of themselves and the people around them, as they should.

But when people fall short of those expectations, the way leaders handle their disappointment can mean the difference between a return to high performance and a downward spiral of failure.

This is a serious deficit I have seen in many otherwise strong leaders. They're inspiring when things go well, but when the numbers slip, they lose their temper or withdraw.

"I need to hold people accountable." I often hear from leaders who lean hard on people when they show disappointing results. "Maybe I yell a little, but they're senior enough to take it."

Sure, maybe. But what's the goal – punishment for the past or performance in the future? There's a massive difference.

Yes, it's important that people are accountable for their results – a few chapters ago I discussed strategies for creating real accountability. But when leaders talk about "holding someone accountable," they don't mean it the way we've been talking about it, what they really mean is "someone needs to be punished."

The truth is, it's very rare that someone needs to be punished. In reality, if they're generally high performers, they already know that they're falling short. And, almost always, they take it seriously.

So what does someone need after a failure? Enough direction and confidence to refocus their energy and take necessary risks to succeed after a failure.

If you're a high-performing impatient leader, supporting others during tough times can be particularly hard for you to do.

It's hard because your natural, knee-jerk response to underperformance is anger, directed at yourself and others. But our natural, knee-jerk responses are often counterproductive. Responding in anger often feels right at the time, but it almost always makes things worse.

So, how should you respond?

1. **Take a breath.** Slow yourself down for the briefest of pauses – just enough time to subvert your default reaction. In that moment, notice your gut reaction. How do you tend to handle poor performance? Do you get angry? Stressed? Needy? Distant? Your goal is to give people what they need to perform, not release what you need to in order to feel better.

2. **Decide on the outcome you want.** In this case it's fairly straightforward: improved performance. Still, be specific. What does this particular person need in order to turn around this particular poor performance or failure? Maybe it's help defining a stronger strategy, or brainstorming different tactics,

or identifying what went right. Maybe they need to know you trust them and you're on their side.

Here's what people almost never need: to feel scared or slapped. And more often than not, that's how we make them feel when we "hold them accountable" in anger.

3. **Choose a response that will achieve the outcome you want, rather than simply making your already obvious displeasure more obvious.**

In hard times, people want to feel more connected to their leaders. Remember everything you read in Element Two: Connecting with Others. People need to trust you and, maybe more important in this situation, they need to feel trusted by you.

But our instinctive response is to be less visible and to communicate less positively. We have to counteract that instinct and connect more. That means more conversations among senior executives, as well as between senior executives and the rest of the organization.

One CEO I know resisted his urge to come down hard on people after a difficult year when the company didn't achieve its goals. He had done that in the past with poor results. We talked about how the employees were already feeling down, compounded by the fact that none of them made the bonus threshold. He wanted to reinvigorate them so he did a counterintuitive thing: He rewarded them.

He told them that, although they didn't earn their bonuses because of the results, he and the other senior executives knew how hard everyone worked. Then he announced that the senior executive team was going to give a share of their compensation to the rest of the company. The new energy and loyalty this created drove the company's turnaround.

Another CEO I know had a meeting scheduled with a project team responsible for a high-profile pilot project that held the possibility of a large piece of client work. But the team was struggling and the pilot faced many challenges, some of them the fault of the team. He had prepared a short speech to tell them how critical this project was, how the company was riding on it, and how they had better fix the problems and make it work or else ...

But after we spoke, he took a chance and changed his tactic. He knew he needed their positive, focused energy now more than ever. And he *did* trust them. He started the way he had intended: "This project is critically important to our success," and then he shifted his approach, "I know you're doing everything you possibly can to make this successful. I want this pilot to succeed. It's imperative. But if we don't get this, it's okay. We'll get others. I believe in you and I trust that you are doing everything possible. Thank you."

They doubled down their efforts and turned the pilot around, eventually winning the larger project.

ELEMENT FOUR

CULTIVATE EMOTIONAL COURAGE

Build Your Confidence	Connect with Others	Commit to Purpose	**Cultivate Emotional Courage**
• Know Who You Are	• Be Curious and Trusting	• Energize Your Focus	• **Feel Courageously**
• Become Who You Want To Be	• Be Clear and Trustworthy	• Focus Their Energy	• **Act Boldly**

As you've been building your confidence, connecting with others, and committing to a larger purpose, you have simultaneously been developing your emotional courage. It is impossible not to. In order to have hard conversations, listen to people's feedback (especially if you didn't respond defensively), help people feel seen and heard, commit to – and rally others around – what's most important to you, you must have felt innumerable feelings: fear, anxiety, thrill, embarrassment, uncertainty, joy, anger, annoyance, frustration, pride, shame, and so much more. Acting in the face of all of those feelings is a huge accomplishment. That is what it means to have emotional courage. And that is what brings you the freedom to be big and do big things. In this section you're going to hone your emotional courage to a master level.

If you are willing to feel everything, you can do anything.

In Part One, Feel Courageously, you will delve more deeply into feeling. The chapters in this part will increase your self-awareness to identify what you're feeling, and even where in your body you're feeling it. With the support and guidance of stories and advice, you will feel everything. Pain and pleasure, joy and sadness, clarity and uncertainty. In growing your familiarity and tolerance for all these feelings, you will be growing your skill, competence, and freedom to feel whatever you must feel in order to follow through and get massive traction on your most important work.

In Part Two, Act Boldly, you will apply that skill, competence, and freedom to act by taking smart, intentional, strategic risks. Risk taking is the doorway to getting movement on what's most important to you, and the chapters in this part will help you increase your capacity to take risks. These chapters will guide you to make decisions you may have been procrastinating, speak truth that is sitting inside you waiting to be spoken, learn new ways of showing up, and risk the vulnerability of an open heart. The more comfortable you become with risk, the more likely you are to make what's most important to you happen.

PART ONE

FEEL COURAGEOUSLY

CHAPTER 37

KNOW WHAT YOU ARE FEELING

DEVELOP YOUR AWARENESS

Over the 30 years since we met, my wife Eleanor and I have spent considerable time, money, and energy on our development. Individually and together, we've taken workshops, studied meditation, practiced yoga, written in journals, talked about our dreams, participated in training programs, and gone to therapy.

A few weeks ago, we were taking a walk along a rural road, questioning why we do it. Is all this inner work simply navel gazing? Or does it impact our lives in a real way?

Just as we were exploring the question, we turned a bend and heard a loud party at a house on the side of the road. As we approached the house we could see the deck was filled with about a dozen college-aged men joking around and drinking.

My body tensed and my emotions intensified. I felt a mix of fear, insecurity, competitiveness, and jealousy. I saw them as the kinds of guys Eleanor would be attracted to – big, alpha, confident – and I felt inferior – which made me feel aggressive toward them. It took me about a minute to realize what I was feeling and why.

I turned to Eleanor and told her what I was feeling. She laughed; she also felt aggressive and had an immediate, instinctual, emotional response, but the opposite of mine. She saw them as obnoxious, uncaring, sexist, and unattractive. She felt superior to them. And resentful that they would probably end up having power in our world.

Two seemingly simple but actually incredibly difficult and crucially important things happened in those few seconds: We recognized what we were feeling, and we talked about it.

Simply being willing to acknowledge a feeling can take courage. We often spend considerable unconscious effort ignoring what we feel because it can be painful. Who wants to be afraid or jealous or insecure? So we stifle the feelings, argue ourselves out of them, or distract ourselves with busy work or small talk.

But just because we don't recognize a feeling doesn't mean it goes away. In fact, it's just the opposite. Not feeling something guarantees it *won't* go away.

Unacknowledged feelings simmer under the surface, waiting to lunge at unsuspecting, undeserving bystanders. Your manager doesn't answer an e-mail, which leaves you feeling vulnerable – though you don't acknowledge it – and then you end up yelling at an employee for something unrelated. Why? Because your anger is coiled in your body, primed, tense, aching to get out. And it's a lot safer to yell at an employee than bring up an uncomfortable complaint with a manager.

This is a particularly pernicious problem in our hyper-efficient, productivity-focused workplaces, where it often feels risky to feel any emotion at all. We're expected to get over things, focus on the work, and not get distracted.

But repression is not an effective strategy. It's where passive aggressiveness is born. It's the foundation of most dysfunctional organizational politics. And it undermines the accountability and action we've been working to create.

A woman I work with interrupted a presentation I was giving in front of 60 people, told me I was approaching it wrong, and directed me to proceed differently. I made a snap decision not to get into a fight on stage and proceeded the way she asked. The presentation went fine.

But she didn't need to interrupt me; the presentation would have gone fine either way. I was angry. I felt stepped on. And I believed she prioritized her own agenda over our mutual one.

I wanted to get back at her. I wanted to embarrass her the way I felt embarrassed. I wanted to talk to lots of other people about her and what she did, gaining their sympathy and support. I wanted to feel better.

But I didn't do anything right away. And, as I sat with the feeling, I realized that while I felt a jumble of emotions, mostly I felt hurt and untrusted.

Mustering up my courage, I e-mailed her, acknowledging the challenge of making in-the-moment decisions but letting her know I felt hurt and mistrusted. She sent me a wonderful e-mail back, acknowledging her mistake and thanking me for my willingness to let her know that she missed the mark.

And, just like that, all my anger uncoiled and slithered away.

Maybe I got lucky. She could have e-mailed back that I was incompetent, monopolizing the stage, and communicating poorly. But, honestly, that would have been fine too, because I would have learned something from it, even if it didn't feel easy in the moment.

Most important to me, our relationship was strengthened by the encounter.

But if I had just railed about her behind her back, built a coalition of support for me and outrage about her? It would have felt good in the moment, but, ultimately, it would have hurt her, the organization, and me.

It sounds easy to know what you're feeling and express it. But it takes great courage. I was tempted to write an e-mail to her about my anger, which would have been safer and kept me in a feeling of power. Hurt feels more vulnerable than anger. But being able to communicate my true, vulnerable feelings made all the difference in how we related to each other.

How do you get to those feelings that may feel vulnerable? Take a little time and space to ask yourself what you are feeling. Notice everything you feel and allow yourself to feel everything. Keep asking until you sense something that feels a little risky, a little exposing. That sensation is probably why you're hesitant to feel it and a good sign that you're now ready to communicate.

It's counterintuitive: Wait to communicate until you feel vulnerable communicating. But it's a good rule of thumb.

Had I not talked to Eleanor about what I was feeling when we saw that deck filled with drinking college guys, I would have gotten clingy to her, looking for some reassurance that she loved me. And, if I had not received it – and why should I since she would have no idea what was going on in my head – I would have become distant, resentful, and insecure.

But instead, we just laughed and focused on other, more interesting conversations. Apparently, all that navel gazing really does impact our lives in a real way.

Becoming aware of what you're feeling will help you make better decisions – in the moment and long term. You won't be controlled by forces you cannot see. As you increase your awareness, what you'll notice is that feeling is physical, not conceptual. And mastering your relationship with the physical sensation of your feelings will give you more freedom to act strategically and intentionally under pressure ...

CHAPTER 38

FEELING IS PHYSICAL

DANCE WITH YOUR MONSTER

I knew that I probably shouldn't send the e-mail I had just written. I wrote it in anger and frustration, and we all know that sending an e-mail written in anger and frustration is, well, dumb.

Still, I really wanted to send it. So I forwarded it to a friend, who knew the situation, with the subject line: Should I send this?

She responded almost immediately: Don't send it tonight. If you feel like you need to send it tonight, then I think it is for the wrong reasons. Make sense?

Yep, I responded. Thanks.

Three minutes later I sent it and bcc'd her.

She was flabbergasted: You changed your mind that fast?!?!?

Nope, I responded. My mind is in total agreement with you. But my mind didn't send the e-mail, my emotions did. And they feel so much better!

Most of the time, I'm professional, focused, empathetic, thoughtful, and rational. But that can take effort and, periodically, I lose that control. I might write an inappropriately aggressive e-mail. Or raise my voice at my kids when they don't listen. Or lose my temper with a customer service rep on the phone who seems to be missing my point.

In those moments, my rational mind doesn't stand a chance. It's like trying to use intellectual arguments to talk down a stampeding bull.

Reason and feelings speak different languages. Reason is intellectual; feelings are physical. Reason favors words; feelings prefer action. Our minds can advise us all they want, but our bodies have the upper hand.

If you pause to feel your feelings, you will recognize them, quite literally, as energy flowing in your body. We live with that energy all the time, and, typically, it's useful – it's information and it keeps us fresh, connected, and ready for action.

But, periodically – perhaps more than periodically? – our feelings can overpower us and, when that happens, a monster takes over and we can easily lose control of our actions.

Imagine this monster lives in your body and feeds on anger, fear and uncertainty. As those emotions grow, so does the monster. Eventually, the pressure to escape the confines of your body proves too great. At that moment, you open your e-mail, read something that annoys you and BOOM!

The BOOM is not a thought. It's a feeling. A physical sensation.

Here's the interesting thing: After we react to the BOOM, we relax. Sending that angry email felt great. The monster escaped.

But not without consequences: The reaction of the person who received my angry e-mail? That's another story.

The question we need to answer is: How can I release the monster without doing damage in the process?

As I wrote in the last chapter, many of us try to manage or ignore our unpleasant emotions. We attempt to push them down, put them aside, or rise above them. But that's a mistake. Those responses only encourage the monster to grow unfettered and, usually, unnoticed. Eventually, without fully understanding why, we get sick or explode or burn out.

There's a better solution: Don't try to manage your feelings. Dance with them instead.

The monster wants out? Let it out. But do so on your terms. You may need to cope for a moment, just until you can get to a place where you have privacy. Then, when you know there will be no adverse consequences, let the monster have you. Free yourself to kick and scream and punch. Feel what it's like to completely lose control.

Recently I was having a hard time keeping it all together while I was in the car with my three children, whom I love to no end and who are also amazingly skilled at pushing my buttons. I held it together long enough to drop them off at our apartment. Then, when I was alone in the car, I let the monster take over. I yelled and cursed and screamed and hit the steering wheel over and over again.

It wasn't pretty. Anyone looking at me through the window would have thought I was crazy. But by the time I returned to the apartment, I felt completely rejuvenated. And, most importantly, I was able to be a good parent.

I've yelled into the woods, repeatedly slammed my fists into my mattress, and jumped up and down stomping on the ground like an infuriated five year old. In places where people might be nearby, like office spaces, airplanes, or hotels, I've gone to the bathroom to have quieter hissy fits, jumping up and down and shaking without letting my voice rise too high.

I know it sounds weird but try it. It feels great. If you pay attention, you can even pinpoint where in your body the monster is living (it may be different each time). As you move the energy, you will notice the physical sensation of your feelings move through your body. Up and out.

If you really can't get any privacy, then, instead of e-mail, open your word processing program and write everything you'd like to say in that angry e-mail. Let yourself go, punching the keys hard as you type, using all the pissy language you'd like to. Let the monster roam free.

Then delete the file, straighten your clothing, and be professional.

The point is to create an intentional and safe doorway for the monster to escape before it explodes. You are physically moving the energy of your feelings, on your terms.

It wasn't long before I received a response from the person to whom I had sent my angry e-mail, and she was clearly annoyed. I had flexed my muscles and she flexed hers back. This time, though, I was prepared. I went into another room, where I was alone, and shouted and jumped and punched into the air. After a few short moments, I felt powerful and balanced. Then I did what I should have done in the first place: I picked up the phone, called her, and had a reasonable conversation.

Once you feel the physical nature of feelings, you can relate to it more simply, as just another sensation. It doesn't need to overpower you. In fact, you might even learn to enjoy it...

CHAPTER 39

PRACTICE FEELING

EMBRACING TEMPTATION

"Oh this is delicious, Peter. The ice cream is homemade, the perfect consistency. And this lemon cookie on top, mmmmm. Are you sure you don't want some?"

Tom smiled mischievously as he reached across the table to hand me a spoon. Tom is my client, the CEO of a technology company. We've worked together for almost a decade and he's become a close, trusted friend.

We were at Greens in San Francisco, a vegetarian restaurant Tom had chosen because he had seen their cookbooks on my shelf in New York and knew I would love it.

Tom was teasing me because earlier in the meal I told him I was off sugary desserts. There's no medical reason or necessity for me to avoid sugar; I simply feel better when I'm not eating it. But he's seen me eat large quantities of sugary treats in the past and knows my willpower can be weak.

"It does look good and I'm glad you're enjoying it," I said, "but you're on your own. There's no chance I'm eating any."

"C'mon Peter, these desserts are healthy, and all we've eaten is vegetables anyway. It would be a real missed opportunity if you didn't at least taste the desserts at Greens; it's your favorite kind of food."

He took a bite from a second dessert he had ordered just to tantalize me – a berry pie – and rolled his eyes in mock ecstasy, "Ooh, this is good. And it's basically just fruit. Go ahead, have just a bite." As he edged it closer to my side of the table, the red caramelized berries dripped juice over the side of the plate.

The reasons to taste the desserts were compelling. Even putting aside the fact that Tom is a client and there's always some pressure to please clients, his rationalizations were the same rationalizations that were floating inside my head.

The more I listened to him, and the longer I looked at the desserts, the more I felt my desire to eat the dessert. I could physically feel the longing. From the tip of my tongue to the depths of my stomach, I craved the sweetness of that dessert. But I didn't give in.

Here's the secret: The only way to face down temptation is to tolerate feeling.

Just think of why we give in to temptation: In order to avoid suffering through the feeling of wanting, we satisfy our desire and, presto, no more feeling. Once I eat the dessert, I will no longer feel the desire to eat the dessert. The desire will have been fulfilled; the tension will have dissipated, we released the monster we met in the last chapter.

It's why we break our diets. It's why we lose our temper. It's why we gossip. The tension of what we're feeling, in the moment, feels too much. So we release the tension – and the feeling – by giving in to the temptation.

The more Tom pressured me to eat dessert, and the longer I held out, the more I felt, which, counterintuitively, strengthened my resolve not to eat the dessert.

This, it turns out, is a great practice for honing your emotional courage. It will grow your capacity to stay with hard feelings; make a commitment and then let others try to entice you into breaking it.

Here's why. Going into the dinner, I had one reason I didn't want to eat dessert. But Tom's taunting gave me another reason: I was embarrassed to break my commitment in the face of his teasing. I didn't want to be the guy who caves in to peer pressure.

Maybe it's just my rebellious nature, but when Eleanor reminds me that I don't really want to eat that cookie in my hand, I quickly try to stuff it in my mouth before she can stop me. Even though I've asked her to help me, my feeling is, "I'll eat whatever I want to eat!" It becomes a fun game, a challenge. Somehow, when she's helping me, I become a little less accountable.

But when Tom was egging me on, the tables were turned. I was fully responsible for my own actions. I knew I was on my own. And I also knew that the stakes were high: If I ate the dessert I would never live it down. The brilliance of the psychology is that Tom made it more fun – and free-spirited – to not eat dessert. And successfully withstanding his pressure built my confidence in my commitment.

This approach has broad application. Do you want to speak less in meetings? Try asking a colleague to egg you on. Want to leave work at a decent time? Have someone prod you at 5 p.m., reminding you of your incomplete to-do list. Trying to stay off e-mail at night? Stare at your phone right before bed and don't touch it (that may be the hardest challenge!).

There are two conditions necessary to make this an effective strategy and keep it good-natured: The commitment you want to make needs to be self-motivated and the person doing the ribbing needs to be a trusted friend who doesn't abuse positional power.

What happens when the prodding is over? Two things: One, you will have grown your emotional courage muscle, and two, you will be more motivated in your commitment.

In my case, the motivating impact of that dinner lasted long after dinner was done. It was a few months before I ate sugar again – months that included a week-long vacation with Eleanor in France – months filled with opportunities to eat delicious-looking sugary treats.

But each time I was tempted, I paused, felt the tension of unsatisfied longing, and knew that I could tolerate the feeling.

I also remembered the dinner with Tom and thought to myself, "if I didn't eat dessert then – with all that pressure and temptation and lots of good reasons to eat dessert – why would I eat it now?"

Tolerating that feeling of temptation requires (and, as a result, builds) emotional courage. If I couldn't tolerate feeling the temptation, then I would eat the dessert. But once I was willing to feel the feelings of wanting it, then I could choose not to have it.

By being aware of what you're feeling, tuning in to the physical sensation of your feelings, and tolerating (even enjoying) those feelings, you're building your capacity to feel. Now let's become more intimate with a few feelings that are unavoidable as you move forward in your most important work, starting with uncertainty ...

CHAPTER 40

FEEL UNCERTAINTY

THE EMOTIONAL ADVENTURE OF LEADERSHIP

I was lost.

I looked at the map and my heart raced as I admitted to myself – only to myself – that I had no idea where I was. It felt too humiliating to let the others know.

This was the summer of 1990 and I was leading a group of students on a 30-day mountaineering expedition. It was the first day of our trip and the students had no experience in the outdoors. They were relying on me. My anxiety level had been creeping up and was now at full tilt.

We were already one hour late for our rendezvous with two other groups with whom we planned to camp and we had been hiking for about three hours. Where were we?

My uneasiness grew as I looked at my watch and realized I was running out of time. The sun would be setting soon and it was dangerous to go on much longer. We would have to make camp while we still had light.

I bit my nails as I looked obsessively from the map to the mountain range and back to the map. We weren't in immediate danger – we had plenty of water and plenty of food – but I was ashamed. My hands shook nervously and I could feel my heart beating.

Thirty minutes later we hit snow. In July. Which, though not uncommon at a certain altitude, confirmed that we were far off track and we needed to set up camp. The jig was up.

I decided to risk the truth.

I gathered the students in a circle and told them we would have to set up camp by ourselves on the snow, and that we would find the other groups in the morning.

"So, we're lost?" a student asked me.

I felt so lame and inadequate. This was not at all what I had thought it would feel like to lead. Leaders are supposed to have the answers. We're supposed to be confident, self-assured, and knowledgeable. We're supposed to know where we are and where we're going at all times.

But here is what I have discovered in my subsequent decades of leadership experience: Leadership is, as much as anything, an emotional adventure.

If you want to be a powerful leader, you have to become familiar with the sweat-inducing, anxiety-producing, adrenaline-generating emotions of being lost while people are following you. Because that is, as often as not, the emotion of leadership.

One of the defining characteristics of strong leaders is their ability to endure uncertainty and ambiguity. They are willing to move through shame and embarrassment and anxiety and fear. Those are the feelings of leadership as much as courage, persistence, and faith. In fact, it's because those feelings are ever-present that we need courage, persistence, and faith.

It takes tremendous confidence to lead. Not the confidence of having all the answers – that's arrogance – but the confidence to move forward even without the answers. You have to be capable of feeling awkward and uncertain without giving up. You have to believe that you and your team have what it takes to see yourselves through – or, if need be, to pick yourselves up and start again. You have to feel courageously.

Here's what not to do: Pretend you're in control. Because that erodes trust, increases your shame, and robs those around you of the opportunity to step in, learn, and help.

"Yes, we're lost," I admitted, "And, to be honest, I'm really embarrassed. But we'll be fine. We'll find the other two groups in the morning. Let's use this as an opportunity to learn how to camp on snow."

I wish I could say that erased my anxiety. It didn't. I stayed anxious until I actually found the other groups the next day and figured out where I had gone wrong.

But coming out of hiding did ease my suffering. And that night turned out to be an exciting bonding experience for everyone on the trip. It gave us – all of us – the confidence that, even though we could get lost, we would also find our way.

Becoming used to uncertainty, and the vulnerability that comes along with it, is an important step in cultivating your emotional courage. There's another emotion that's equally unavoidable if you want to lead powerfully: pain. Your willingness to feel pain takes courage and offers ultimate freedom to be yourself and do what's most important ...

CHAPTER 41

BE WILLING TO FEEL
THE HARD STUFF

WHY LEADERS MUST FEEL PAIN

I was on a plane, flying back to New York from California where I'd spent the week in Ann Bradney's intense leadership workshop I've referenced a few times in this book.

In the aisle across from me, a mother was sitting with her two daughters, one about five years old, the other about seven. I happened to look over as the mom was working with the younger daughter on a math problem. I listened for a moment and soon found it hard to breathe.

She was furious at the girl for not knowing the answers to her math problems: "Why don't you know that? What are you learning in school? All you do is watch TV!"

The little girl began to cry. When she did, her mom's fury escalated. She hammered on, through the girl's tears, with a word problem: "If you buy candy for $1.00 and a drink for $1.25, how much do you have to pay? Well? How much do you have to pay?" Her little girl turned her head away, sobbing.

At that point, I started to tear up too.

Mostly, I cried for the girl, but also for her mother. I don't know what pain this woman has felt in her life or what drives her anger. But I know it's not her child's inability to solve a math problem.

And I would not be at all surprised if she'd endured similar treatment when she was her daughter's age.

I realized that I was also crying for my own mother, for myself, and for my children. When I was a child, I felt what that girl was feeling. And, as an adult, I have grown angry with my children for not knowing things.

Here's the thing: When we avoid feeling the suffering we naturally experience as human beings, we perpetuate it and act against our best interests (and the best interests of others) in our relationships with our colleagues and the people we manage, as well as with our families.

The act of diving deeply into the feelings we avoid, the feelings we don't necessarily even know we have, is, I have come to believe, our only hope of breaking our link in the chain of hurt, suffering, and ineffectiveness. It's what we've been doing throughout this book.

And it's what we did in Ann's leadership workshop. One CEO in the group talked about how, even though she knows her team is capable, she avoids delegating. And now she is exhausted from carrying the weight of her company, saving everyone from making mistakes, and doing their work for them.

Here's where it got interesting: She didn't just talk about her exhaustion; she felt it. She lay on a mattress, was physically held by others in the group, and cried. Soon, she began to speak about her brother who killed himself years earlier. Through tears, she told us of her feelings of helplessness at not being able to save him.

It soon became evident that, unable to save her brother, she is trying to save everyone else, a habit that is draining her and could prevent her company from succeeding.

This is not a leadership *skills* issue. She already knows everything there is to learn about delegation. But until she faces – not just intellectually, but physically and emotionally – that she couldn't save her brother, all the delegation skills in the world will not help her.

At this point, you may be rolling your eyes at the California-ness of all of this. A leadership workshop with crying? Touching? Extreme self-disclosure?

But that's the point, really. Talking about emotions doesn't get us very far. That's the shortcoming of teaching emotional intelligence as a skill. It doesn't go far enough. To really become emotionally intelligent, emotionally mature, we have to experience the emotions.

Over the five days of the workshop, there were countless examples of ways in which each of us were stuck in self-defeating patterns. And each time, the cause of the habit had deep origins, born from suffering that was too heavy for us to carry with the maturity we had at the time we experienced it. These feelings are deeply embedded in our bodies as well as our minds. Years of traditional therapy do not unlock them. But we need to release them.

The solution? Feel courageously. Feel all your feelings, deeply. Especially the painful ones.

We need to surround ourselves by others who are supportive, loving, and courageous, and then dive back into the one pool in which we really don't want to swim – the painful feelings of both the past and the present – and realize that we won't drown. Sometimes it feels like drowning. But every one of us emerged from Ann's workshop feeling more alive than when we entered it.

I have spent my life trying to prove that I'm good enough to live it. As I mentioned earlier in this book, my mother narrowly escaped the holocaust, and her baby sister Ariel did not survive. I grew up thinking daily of the six million Jews killed by the Nazis, thinking that because of them, my life had better amount to something.

And now I watch myself drop names of important people I know and talk too much about things I've accomplished. I brag, too often striving more for my own success than the success of others, or of endeavors I believe in.

This is a destructive game. The more I try to impress others, the less I believe in myself. And no amount of communication training will help unless I can feel the pain of never feeling good enough and acknowledge that my life can never make up for any of the six million. The only way we can move forward, live fully, and lead courageously, is by feeling enough to become deeply mature human beings.

We cannot lead without feeling the pain of living because the things we do to avoid feeling pain result in poor leadership and constricted living. We don't acknowledge others. We try to control everything. We lose our temper and criticize others disproportionately.

If we don't feel our emotions, we are controlled by them.

Toward the end of the flight, the mother had fallen asleep, and the girl was snuggled against her peacefully. How much better would it be if her mother could offer that comfort awake?

How much more powerful would the CEO be if she could convey her trust in her very capable people, delegating with the confidence that they will accomplish their tasks?

And how much better of a father, husband, writer, and leader would I be if I could speak and write the truth as I see it without worrying about how it would make me look?

My heart is beating hard as I write this and think about exposing the sides of me that brag and cry. It feels scary but also powerful. It feels like leadership.

The picture I'm painting of myself – of you – is complex. We are many things – often contradictory – all at the same time. That's the complicated truth of being a human being. And, the best way to meet that complicated truth, is to uncompromisingly, unhesitatingly, unshamefully, feel it all ...

CHAPTER 42

FEEL EVERYTHING

ALLOW FOR COMPLEXITY

Hurricane Sandy was barreling toward the coast and the news reports were grim. This would be the worst storm to hit the Northeast region since, well, maybe ever. A confluence of factors – it was slow-moving, widespread, clashing with a winter storm from the west and cold air from the north, and hitting land at high tide on a full moon – could lead to disastrous flooding, loss of power for millions, billions of dollars in damages, and lost lives.

Meanwhile, my kids were delighted.

When it became clear over the weekend that school would be closed Monday, they squealed with joy and started to make plans for how to spend the time – how much TV they were going to watch, how much candy they were going to eat. They bubbled with excitement as we got ready by shopping for food and supplies, filling bottles with water, putting candles in each room, and connecting with neighbors. We listened to news reports and tracked the storm on the Internet. The city was abuzz as people prepared.

As we now know, the hurricane did, indeed, wreak devastation. When I booted up my computer – I was lucky and did not even lose power – I saw that tunnels were flooded, a massive fire destroyed 50 houses in Rockaway, and power was out for millions. I cried as I read that a tree fell on a house in Westchester and killed two boys, one 11, the other 13.

And still, at the same time, I remember hearing my kids outside my home office, laughing as they played freeze tag and hide and seek, enjoying another day off school. I remember – even in the face of the horror I was reading about – how it made me smile.

This is not a simple story. I did not feel one emotion after the next. I felt both pain and joy – not in equal measures, but simultaneously.

Here's what makes it even more complicated: The joy I felt was not relief from realizing that I escaped the devastation – though I felt that too.

Both the sadness and happiness I felt are because of the hurricane – sadness about the devastation and joy from the day I got to spend with my kids. I feel callous writing this.

But that is the reality of emotions and of life. The same event can often catalyze conflicting feelings.

Some people in your company get laid off and you might feel sadness, anger, and frustration at the loss while also feeling relief that you are not among them. All those are easy emotions to accept. But you might also feel excitement at the opportunity you may now have to step into someone else's role. Or joy at seeing someone you never liked leave the company.

And then you might feel shame that you feel joy and excitement. In fact, you might feel so much shame that you don't admit – even to yourself – that you feel the joy and excitement because it doesn't seem right to feel pleasure about something that causes pain for others.

Here's the problem though: Repressed feelings leak out in inappropriate and insidious ways. Remember, feelings are energy, and if you don't acknowledge them, they lock up in your body and reappear, often in disguise.

One disguise is physical pain. You feel a crick in your neck, your back hurts, or you get sick. But that's not a repressed emotion's only trick.

Someone else expresses excitement at the opportunity that the layoff has afforded her and you respond in overwhelming anger at her insensitivity. Why? Maybe because she is being insensitive. But if your anger is a little over the top, consider that perhaps you feel shame at sharing her feelings. And, since you want to distance yourself from your feelings, you distance yourself from her.

You label her as lacking compassion, uncaring, cold. You no longer trust her. And then you lose an opportunity with her. Maybe you lose a friend. And you further distance yourself from your own feelings, pushing them deeper inside, increasing the probability that you will get sick or angry again, alienating more people.

There is an alternative and it is the skill of living well and living fully: Feel everything.

One feeling does not negate another feeling; it just complicates it. The pleasure I feel at having a day with my family and watching their excitement does not diminish the pain I feel at devastation left in the wake of the storm. It just complicates it.

Here's the key: Feeling everything does not mean expressing everything.

It is completely appropriate – even crucial – to feel everything. But that does not mean that it's appropriate to share it indiscriminately with the people around you. So what should you do?

1. **Feel – and acknowledge to yourself – everything you feel.** And feel it deeply. Don't censor anything. It is unusual to feel a single, simple emotion. Usually emotions come muddled together: pain and pleasure, joy and sadness, excitement and fear. Risk feeling it all without censoring any of it. Recognize that your rational mind may not be able to sort it all out and let go of the need for it to make sense or feel good.

2. **Know who you can trust with your full and complicated self and trust them.** We all need at least one person in our lives with whom we can truly be ourselves. Someone who will not judge you and whose opinion of you will only deepen as you reveal yourself more fully. For some, that person will be your spouse or partner or close friend. If you don't have someone like that, consider taking the risk of revealing

yourself more fully to someone who you might be able to trust or consider a coach or a therapist who is trained to help you accept and integrate all that you feel. What's most important is that you don't censor yourself.

3. **Think about your audience before sharing your feelings.** This is always a good idea but especially important with complicated and conflicting feelings. First of all, everyone is in a different situation and will have different feelings. If someone has been recently laid off, he will almost certainly – and appropriately – resent any positive feeling you have. Also, not everyone will be as brave with feeling as you. Many people repress their own feelings and then lash out at you for accepting yours. If you're not sure about your audience, it's better to say little or nothing at all. Here, it's not only appropriate – it's smart – to censor yourself.

On the day after the hurricane, I joined my children for a walk through Central Park to ogle at the trees that fell and to witness the ravages of the storm. I shared with them my pain thinking about the suffering that people were experiencing, my gratitude that we escaped the worst of it, and my awareness that our position of relative privilege in the world gave us a warm safe house that protected us. And I also shared their laughter as we joked and played in the rain, splashing through puddles and enjoying a day off together from school.

It feels risky to write and publish this. As with the last chapter, I am afraid that I will be judged for it.

But that's the point, right? And I am more afraid of the alternative. Of living in a world where only some emotions are acceptable while the others must be stuffed deep down, until our acceptable, acknowledged selves are finally overwhelmed by our ravaged, intolerable, ignored selves, and we either explode or self-destruct.

And so I feel. And I write. And I publish.

PART TWO

ACT BOLDLY

CHAPTER 43

RISK IS THE KEY TO LEADERSHIP

UNLOCKING YOUR SUCCESS EQUATION

Jim Wolfensohn was a second-year student at the University of Sydney when a friend of his and the captain of the fencing team, Rupert Bligh, asked if he wanted to go to Melbourne the next day to fence in the national university championships.

"You've got to be crazy," Jim said. "I've never fenced in my life."

Rupert wasn't crazy, just desperate. A member of the team had fallen ill and they needed a replacement to qualify for the event.

It was an insane idea. Jim had no money for the trip to Melbourne and no chance of success.

But he said yes, borrowed the money from his parents, and learned what he could from his new teammates on the train to Melbourne.

What a wonderful story this would be if it ended with Jim uncovering a hidden, inborn talent and vanquishing all his opponents. But that's not this story. Jim lost every bout and failed to score a single point.

Still, he said, "I tried to invent new ways to score points on the opponent. I could not remember having such a good time ever before."

Even with his losses, the team won the championship. And Jim stuck with fencing for years, eventually fencing in the 1956 Olympics and becoming President of the World Bank, a position he held from 1995 to 2005.

Wait, what? What does Jim's fencing experience have to do with his esteemed business and political career? Everything.

Every life story is complex, with an infinite number of factors contributing to a person's fate. And yet, there are patterns, ways in which we habitually interact with our experiences. Over time, those patterns become our destinies.

For most of us, our patterns can be seen early in our lives. Jim's patterns – the ones that led him to great personal, business, and political success – were already clear in his failed fencing bouts.

First, some disclosure: I've known Jim most of my life and have always admired him, not just for his accomplishments, but also for his integrity as a person and as a leader. He's always been on my short list of people I want to be like when I grow up. I'm still working on it.

So what's the pattern behind Jim's success?

Psychologists might focus on his upbringing. He grew up poor and developed the dynamic combination of insecurity and ambition that underlies so many stories of achievement.

Life coaches might point to his willingness to agree to opportunities that are larger than he could handle – often without even really knowing what he was getting into – and then to work tirelessly to succeed, accepting help wherever he could find it.

Sure, consultants might offer, that's part of it. But the real source of his success is his analytical mind and the disciplined way he solves problems. He enters a situation and assesses it, seeking to understand the system and figure out what's getting in the way. He identifies the smallest number of actions that will have the biggest impact, and he follows through.

It's his optimism, positive psychologists would likely suggest. How else could he say, after losing every bout, "I could not remember having such a good time ever before." And his relationships gave him opportunities, as well. He never would have fenced if not for Rupert offering him a place on the team.

Yes, but he would not have been able to achieve anything if he were not capable, his professors at Harvard would argue. Jim is smart and skilled. He works hard. And he never stops learning. The story of his fencing trip to Melbourne is dramatic, but his success as a fencer – and as a business and world leader – is hidden in the long stretch between that bout and the Olympics. He spent years working hard, honing his skills, and increasing his talent.

Maybe Jim's pattern is really an equation: Jim = integrity + insecurity + ambition + saying yes + asking for help + problem solving + optimism + relationships + capability. Like I said, every life story is complex.

But the more I think about Jim, the more clearly I see simplicity in his success. A single underlying force drove his decision-making. It's the key that unlocked his equation. Without it, his tremendous talent would have lain dormant.

That key is a question.

Most people, when they explore an opportunity, next step, or decision, ask, "Will I succeed?"

But Jim asks a different question: "Is it worth the risk?"

The difference in those questions is the difference between never fencing at all and fencing in the Olympics. When Rupert asked Jim to fence in the championships, there's no chance he could have succeeded. Failure was the inevitable outcome. But was it worth the risk? For Jim, it certainly was.

Jim's approach to life is to take a risk, learn from it, and take his new knowledge and understanding to the next risk. Failure is an essential part of his strategy.

Really taking risks requires failing. You have to fear failure enough to work hard to make the risks pan out successfully, but not so much that you don't take the risks in the first place.

Viewed through the lens of learning, failure is at least as beneficial as success. Working only on things you're pretty sure will work significantly limits what you can achieve. Instead, take risks. And then see what happens.

Your success equation may differ from Jim's. But the key that unlocked his success equation – the willingness to pursue reasonable, thoughtful, intentional risks – is a master key. It will unlock your success as well.

So, how do you increase your ability and willingness to take smart risks? By building your risk muscle ...

CHAPTER 44

BUILD YOUR RISK MUSCLE

THE SMALL PERSONAL RISKS THAT CHANGE BEHAVIOR

One of the things I love about my synagogue is its commitment to inclusiveness. The community welcomes people of all faiths and integrates practices from other traditions.

One year, on Yom Kippur, the Day of Repentance, the most solemn day in the Jewish calendar, after several hours of prayer, I felt an impulse to do something that is never done in a traditional synagogue. I wanted to take my shoes and socks off. In the Eastern spiritual traditions that inform my yoga and meditation practice, bare feet is seen as respectful and helpful to centered, grounded meditation and prayer. But the idea of doing it in a synagogue scared me.

I rationalized my reticence with a number of reasonable excuses: The gentleman sitting to my right was impeccably and formally dressed – handkerchief in his breast pocket and all – what would he think? I didn't want to disrupt his experience and I didn't want to feel his judgment. Also, I was in the front row, visible to many congregants, and I am a member of the board. What would others think? What would the Rabbi think? What would it look like for a board member to be barefoot in synagogue? Better not risk it, I thought.

Then I saw Jonathan.

He had been given the honor of opening the Ark to remove the Torah, Judaism's holiest book. This is arguably the most visible moment in the service. Everyone is paying attention. And, as Jonathan walked to the stage, I couldn't help but laugh. He was barefoot.

Instantly, I knew it was okay for me to be barefoot. I was still worried I would look stupid, still concerned about the judgment of others. But seeing someone else take a braver risk than I was contemplating made me more willing to take my smaller risk.

And so I took off my shoes.

We often think of leadership in big, dramatic ways: ambitious visions, well-articulated strategies, convincing speeches, compelling conversations.

Those things can be useful tools for a powerful leader. But they are not the essence of leadership. The essence of leadership is having the courage to show up differently than the people around you. That's it. It's simple.

Most people I know – myself included – stop short of what we can accomplish because, frankly, we're scared. Of looking bad. Of failing. Of being humiliated. We're hiding, unwilling to be vulnerable, unsure whether to take a risk. But leadership calls us to step forward first and take the risk that others are afraid to take.

I was in a meeting with a number of senior executives who were all blaming each other for the company's lackluster revenue numbers. The goal of the meeting was to uncover the causes and each person was pointing to someone else's division as the source of the problem. The head of sales blamed marketing for targeting the wrong prospects. Marketing blamed operations for pricing the product noncompetitively. Operations blamed the company's technology for being too cumbersome and expensive.

Then the head of customer service spoke up.

He started by saying that the problems the company was facing were complex but he could think of at least three ways that he contributed to making them worse. His department wasn't prioritizing the most critical customers, they weren't effectively funneling information they were gathering from customers to the rest of the organization, and, maybe the biggest problem of all, he had morale issues in his group. Then he listed things he was planning to do to address those three issues.

After he spoke, there was silence in the room. Then, one by one, the others started claiming their part in the problems.

That's barefoot leadership.

Barefoot leadership is about acting in ways that change the way others act. It's about taking a risk that others are scared to take – having hard conversations, creating accountability, and inspiring action – in a way that shifts a room, a team, or even the culture of an organization.

One of my clients, a technology company, was having quality issues in some of their products. Quarter after quarter, the executive team had committed to solving the problems. But, when forced to choose, they always decided to ship a slightly flawed product in order to make their quarterly numbers, rather than take the sales hit.

The CEO and I discussed the negative reinforcing pattern of this consistent choice and, one day, the CEO declined a high profile sale that would have added millions to his top line, because it was clear that the product would ship with quality issues.

"Wait," his head of sales argued, "We can ship it and make repairs in the field." Everyone agreed – the SVPs of operations, engineering, even HR. The CEO was under intense pressure from his team to give in, but he held his ground. Everyone's bonuses that year – including the CEO's – were lower as a result.

That was the last year the company had serious quality issues.

That's barefoot leadership.

This doesn't just apply to CEOs and other top executives. Anyone who is willing to take a risk publicly – even a small one – stands as an example for others to follow.

A short while after I took off my shoes, I noticed that the man sitting next to me – the well-dressed one with the handkerchief in his pocket – was looking at my feet. "Oh no," I thought to myself, "here comes the judgment."

To my surprise, he smiled at me and bent over to take off his own shoes and socks. After services, I asked him why he decided to do it.

"When I saw your bare feet, it gave me permission to take my shoes off," he said. Then he quickly added, "Not that I needed permission. Still, you made it easier."

Acting boldly will always bring up feelings that are hard to move through. So we need practice taking risks. A simple way to practice while also stimulating forward momentum is to make some decisions, especially ones you've been procrastinating about ...

CHAPTER 45

MAKE A DECISION

ACT BOLDLY TO GET MOVING

I perused the restaurant menu for several minutes, struggling with indecision, each item tempting me in a different way.

Maybe I should order them all...

Is this a silly decision not deserving deliberation? Maybe. But I bet you've been there – if not about food, then about something else.

We spend an inordinate amount of time, and a tremendous amount of energy, making choices between equally attractive options in everyday situations. The problem is that, although they may be equally attractive, they are also differently attractive, with trade-offs that require compromise. Even when deciding between kale salad (healthy and light), salmon (to stave off hunger), and ravioli (tasty, but high carbs).

If these mundane decisions drag on our time and energy, think about the bigger ones we need to make in organizations all the time. Which products should we pursue and which should we kill? Who should I hire or fire? Should I initiate that difficult conversation?

These questions are followed by an infinite number of other questions. If I am going to have that difficult conversation, when should I do it? And how should I start? Should I call them or see them in person or email them? Should I do it publicly or in private? How much information should I share? And on and on...

So how can we handle decisions of all kinds more efficiently? I have three methods that I use, the first two of which I talk about in my book, *Four Seconds,* and the third of which will ask you to act boldly and will build your risk muscle as a result.

The first method is to use habits as a way to reduce routine decision fatigue. The idea is that if you build a habit – for example, always eat salad for lunch – then you avoid the decision entirely and you can save your decision-making energy for other things.

That works for predictable and routine decisions. But what about unpredictable ones?

The second method is to use if/then thinking to routinize unpredictable choices. For example, let's say someone constantly interrupts me and I'm not sure how to respond. My if/then rule might be: If the person interrupts me two times in a conversation, then I will say something.

These two techniques – habits and if/then – can help streamline many typical, routine choices we face in our lives.

What we haven't solved for are the larger more strategic decisions that aren't habitual and can't be predicted. That's where acting boldly comes in.

The CEO and leadership team at one of my clients was facing a number of unique, one-off decisions, the outcomes of which couldn't be accurately predicted.

These were decisions like how to respond to a competitive threat, in which products to invest more deeply, how to better integrate an acquisition, where to reduce a budget, how to organize reporting relationships, and so on.

These are precisely the kinds of decisions that can linger for weeks, months, or even years, stalling the progress of entire organizations. These decisions are impossible to habitualize and can't be resolved with if/then rules. Most importantly, they are decisions for which there is no clear, right answer.

We tend to perseverate over these sorts of decisions for a long time, collecting more data, excessively weighing pros and cons, soliciting additional opinions, delaying while we wait, hoping for a clear answer to emerge that would increase the payoff and minimize the risk.

But what if we could use the fact that there is no clear answer to make a faster decision?

"It's 3:15 p.m.," the CEO told his leadership team as they were debating what to do with a certain business, "We need to make a decision by 3:30 p.m."

"Hold on," the CFO responded, "this is a complex decision. We should continue the conversation until we come to a clear answer."

"No." The CEO was resolute. "We will make a decision within the next 15 minutes."

And you know what? They did.

They all had to feel the complexity of the emotions we've been talking about – uncertainty, anxiety, fear, accountability, excitement – and then act boldly in the face of those feelings.

Which is how I came to my third decision-making method: Use a timer.

If the issues on the table have been reasonably vetted, the choices are equally attractive, and there is still no clear answer, then admit that there is no clearly identifiable right way to go and just decide.

It helps if you can make the decision smaller, with minimal investment, to test it. But if you can't, then just make the decision. Feel courageously, act boldly. The time you save by not deliberating pointlessly will pay massive dividends in productivity.

Hold on, you may protest. If I do spend more time on it, an answer will emerge. Sure, maybe. But, (1) you've wasted precious time waiting for that clarity and, (2) the clarity of that one decision seduces you to linger, counterproductively and in fruitless hope for clarity, on too many other decisions.

Just decide and move forward.

Try it now. Pick a decision you have been postponing, give yourself three minutes, and just make it. If you are overwhelmed with too many decisions, take a piece of paper and write a list of the decisions. Give yourself a set amount of time and then, one by one, make the best decision you can make in the moment. Making the decision – any decision – will reduce your anxiety and let you move forward. The best antidote to feeling overwhelmed is forward momentum.

As for my lunch, I ordered the kale salad. Was it the best choice? I don't know. But at least I'm not still sitting around trying to order.

While acting boldly requires emotional courage, it also builds your emotional courage. It's a positive, forward moving spiral. One decision I encourage you to make (it may feel like one of your biggest risks, while also being one of the most simple and straightforward): Tell the truth …

CHAPTER 46

RISK TRUTH

IT'S YOUR JOB TO TELL THE BOLD TRUTHS

Rashid, the CEO of a technology company and a client of mine for nearly a decade, called to tell me we had a major issue with some of the newer members of his leadership team.

What comes to mind when you think of what might constitute a "major issue" with some senior leaders? Maybe they're in a fight? Maybe they're making poor strategic decisions? Perhaps they're not following through on commitments they made about the business? Maybe they're being abusive to their employees? Maybe they're stealing?

I've seen all those problems in the past at various companies. But none of that was happening at Rashid's firm. The major issue he was talking about was far more subtle – and in most places even acceptable.

Rashid had heard, through the grapevine, that two new team members were quietly questioning whether they should be honest about the gaps they saw in the business.

Is that really such a big deal? How many of us would prefer to keep the peace and avoid being the naysayer? Or prioritize being seen as a team player over identifying problems that may lie in someone else's department? Or downplay an issue of our own team, hoping we'll be able to fix it before anyone notices?

It's hard to speak up about potentially sensitive issues. But Rashid's company's fast growth and strong results were based, more than anything, on one underlying requirement for anyone in a leadership role: courage.

Courage underlies all smart risk taking – we just saw that in the last chapter related to decisions. No company can grow without leaders who are willing to take risks. And if we can't speak the truth about what we see and what we think, then it's unlikely that we'll take other smart risks necessary to lead.

So, yes, it's a major issue if direct reports to the CEO aren't willing to say what they really think. In fact, I'd say that there's little value to having senior leaders in an organization who don't speak their minds.

It's worth asking if Rashid is creating a safe enough environment for people to speak up. That's a good thing to consider and, in part, it's my job to help him do that.

It's also worth asking if the leaders have the skills to talk about sensitive topics with care and competence. This is important because it does take tremendous skill to raise hard-to-talk-about issues in a way that convinces others to address them. If they don't have the skill, it's easily trainable (give them a copy of this book!).

Ultimately, Rashid is running a company with highly compensated leaders who are running large and complicated businesses of their own, and it's fair for him to expect them to be brave enough to tell him what they are thinking.

How could people, who have been so successful in their careers, not be courageous about communicating the problems they see in a business for which they are responsible?

The biggest challenge we face is rarely about discovering the perfect strategy or developing a smarter product or figuring out the gaps in the business. It's about being courageous enough to take the risks necessary to talk about the difficult, sometimes scary truth.

That's been the secret to Rashid's company's growth and the success of his leadership team. Good leaders almost always know what needs to be done. Great leaders actually do it.

So, Rashid asked, what should I do?

"The answer is simple and straightforward," I said. "You have to talk to them. Be direct about how you believe they're hurting the business. Tell them the bold truth about what you need from them. Lead by example. It's the only way."

Acting boldly most likely means that you are choosing to do something differently than usual (otherwise it wouldn't feel bold). That will bring you to one of your most difficult but inescapable feelings yet – inauthenticity ...

CHAPTER 47

TRY SOMETHING DIFFERENT

THE UNEXPECTED POWER OF INAUTHENTICITY

"Whoa! What are you doing?" I asked aghast.

I had just walked into my daughter's room as she was working on a science project. Normally, I would have been pleased at such a sight. But this time, her project involved sand. A lot of it. And, although she had put some plastic underneath her work area, it wasn't nearly enough. The sand was spreading all over our newly renovated floors.

My daughter, who immediately felt my displeasure, began to defend herself. "I used plastic!" she responded angrily.

I responded more angrily, "But the sand is getting all over!"

"Where else am I supposed to do it?" she yelled.

Why won't she admit when she's done something wrong? I thought to myself. I felt my fear, projecting into the future: What would her life look like if she couldn't own her mistakes?

My fear translated into more anger, this time about how important it was for her to admit mistakes, and we spiraled. She said something that felt disrespectful to me and I raised my voice. She devolved into a crying fit.

I wish I could say this never happened before. But my daughter and I were in a dance, one we have, unfortunately, danced before. And it's predictably painful; we both, inevitably, end up feeling terrible.

This is not just a parenting dance. I often see leaders and managers fall into predictable spirals with their employees, many examples of which you have read in earlier chapters. It usually starts with unfulfilled expectations ("what were you thinking?") and ends in anger, frustration, sadness, and loss of confidence on both sides. Maybe not crying, but the professional equivalent.

I'm always inclined to ask, "Why do I react the way I do?" The answer is a complicated fusion of reasons including my love for my daughter, my desire to teach her, my low tolerance for messiness, my need to be in control, my longing for her success, and the list goes on.

But it doesn't really matter.

Because knowing why I act a certain way does not change my behavior. You would think that it would. It should. But it doesn't.

The question that really matters – the hard question – is how do I change?

First, I need a better way to respond to my daughter. For this, I went to Eleanor, who is truly a master. I asked her how I should have handled it.

"Sweetie," she said, role-playing me in the conversation with my daughter, "There's a lot of sand here and we need to clean it up before it destroys the floors, how can I help?"

Simple and effective:

1. Identify the problem.
2. State what needs to happen.
3. Offer to help.

That's a great way to handle it. Think about any problem you face with someone at work. I don't suggest you start the conversation with "Sweetie," but the rest is applicable.

I watched a manager get angry at a direct report (we'll call him Fred) for a sloppy, unclear presentation he gave. The manager was right – the presentation was unclear – but the way he responded damaged the employee's confidence and Fred's next effort wasn't much better. Instead, he could have tried this:

"Fred, this presentation made six points instead of one or two. I'm left confused. It needs to be shorter, more to the point, and more professional looking. Would it help if we talk about the point you're trying to make?"

No frustration. Not even disappointment. Just clarity and support.

Another time, I watched as a CEO got annoyed at his direct reports for presenting plans that were not reflective of the budget commitments they had made. His emotion was understandable. Appropriate, even. But not useful. An alternative might have been:

"Folks, these plans don't reflect the budget numbers we agreed on. Those numbers are nonnegotiable. If you want, you can let me know where you are getting stuck and we can brainstorm solutions."

Identify the problem. State what needs to happen. Offer to help. Simple, right?

But – and this is the strange part – in my situation, I couldn't bring myself to do it. As I thought about it, I realized my impediment.

It didn't feel authentic.

I believe strongly in leading and living with authenticity. And I was angry and worried about my daughter's future. So responding calmly, in that moment, would represent a disconnect between how I felt and how I acted. That's inauthentic.

And then it hit me: Learning requires emotional courage because, by definition, it will always feel inauthentic.

Practicing a new behavior, showing up in a new way, or acting differently, feels inauthentic. Changing a dance that's been danced many times before will never feel natural. It will feel awkward, fake, like pretending. The hedge fund manager was angry, the CEO was annoyed. Not expressing those emotions feels fake.

But it's much smarter, more likely to compassionately teach the people around us, and a better approach to getting them to reverse their ineffective behaviors.

If we want to learn, we need to tolerate the feeling of inauthenticity long enough to integrate the new way of being, long enough for the new way to feel natural. If the new way works, that happens sooner than you would think.

Yesterday, my daughter was doing homework late at night and I had to ask her to work in the dining room instead of her bedroom because her younger sister needed to go to bed.

But, before I did, I paused. I empathized with the challenges she would feel, being asked to leave her room for her sister. Being asked to do her difficult homework in a place that wasn't as comfortable.

"Sweetie," I said, "Your sister needs to go to sleep and we need to move you into the dining room. How can I help?" Identify the problem, state what needs to happen, and offer to help.

It felt weird. Like I was being overly solicitous. Fake.

But it worked.

After I helped her move, she quickly got back to her work.

Then, as I was walking out, I heard her say "Dad?" I paused at the door and looked back at her. "Thanks," she said, without looking up from her book.

Even now, as I think about that moment, I feel such a delicious feeling of warmth and happiness in my heart. It's the payoff of all this hard work, the payoff of living with confidence, connection, commitment, and courage. The possibilities of what you can create when you integrate the four elements are limitless. And it all comes down to a single moment ...

CHAPTER 48

THE LIMITLESS POSSIBILITY OF NOW

A QUESTION THAT CAN CHANGE YOUR LIFE

For years I've exercised every day – doing weights, cardio, yoga – but despite my continuous effort, I haven't seen much change.

Until a short while ago.

Recently, my body has changed. My muscles are stronger, more defined, and I've lost five pounds along with a visible layer of fat. So what did I do differently?

Let's start with what I didn't do: Spend more time exercising. In fact, I've spent less. What I did change is how I use the time I spend working out.

Instead of doing the same old workout, day after day, I'm mixing it up with new routines. I'm focusing my effort more wisely – confusing my muscles with different exercises, adding balance challenges, power moves, and intervals.

The rapid results I achieved by changing my exercise routine made something very clear to me: We habitually squander time and effort on behaviors that do little to move us toward the outcomes we're seeking. Spending an hour on a treadmill watching TV had no visible impact on my fitness. But when I used that hour differently, I saw improvement.

It's not that we're lazy. We put effort into what we do. I ran on the treadmill every day. But, like my daily run, our efforts often don't translate into optimum results.

The basic principle is simple: We're already spending a certain amount of time doing things—in meetings, managing businesses, writing e-mails, making decisions. If we could just make a higher impact during that time, it's all upside with no cost.

So here's the question I'd like to propose you ask yourself throughout your day: What can I do, right now that would be the most powerful use of this moment?

What can I say? What action can I take? What question can I ask? What issue can I bring up? What decision can I make that would have the greatest impact?

Asking these questions – and answering them honestly – is the path to choosing new actions that could bring better outcomes. The hard part is following through on the answers and taking the risks to reap the full benefits of each moment. That takes bold action. Courage. But it's also what brings the payoff.

I was once sitting in a meeting with the CEO of a large bank and his head of HR. Right before the meeting the CEO had told me that he had lost confidence in his HR chief after he had made a number of blunders without accepting any responsibility. "He really needs to go," the CEO told me.

Then, during the meeting, the head of HR asked the CEO for feedback. He's opened the door, I thought to myself. But the CEO said nothing. That led to more dysfunction as the head of HR stayed on, continuing to disappoint the CEO, but without getting straight feedback.

It's easy to judge the CEO. And he certainly should have been bolder. But how many of us miss similar opportunities out of fear or nervousness or even simply concern for hurting other people's feelings?

Although the CEO's missed opportunity was a glaring omission with painful consequences, it is, unfortunately, not unusual.

There's some good reason for that: Sometimes the bold move can backfire. I know a similar situation to the one I just mentioned, in which a VP-level person asked her employee for feedback, but when the employee answered honestly, he was shunned and treated poorly afterwards.

Rejection, failure, even ridicule – those are the risks of making the most powerful use of a moment. But in my experience, boldness, combined with skilled communication, almost always pays off because it moves the energy of a situation and creates new possibilities in otherwise old ruts.

Having the courage to take the kind of bold action that creates new opportunities is, possibly, the most critical skill a leader – or anyone – can have. The skills to follow through are what you've learned in this book—be confident, connect with others, commit to a larger purpose, and hone your emotional courage.

I recently saw a short video that perfectly illustrates the power of integrating confidence, connection, commitment, and courage and the risk-reward payoff of using a moment well. Billy Joel was speaking at Vanderbilt University when a young student, Michael Pollack, raised his hand. When Joel called on him, Michael asked if he could play the piano to accompany the musician for a song. A silence followed. Michael had taken a big risk just by asking and you could feel the tension and suspense in the room. After a pause, Joel simply said, "Okay," and the video of their astounding spontaneous collaboration has now been viewed millions of times.

How often have you been in a similar situation, at one time or another, wanting to say something or do something, yet letting the moment pass by? Next time you're in that situation, pay attention to it. Notice the feelings that come along with it. Observe the physical sensations in your body. Can you feel your heart beating? Can you connect with the conflicting urges to act and not to? Getting in touch with those feelings is the first step to acting in the face of them.

Woody Allen famously said that 80% of success is showing up. Maybe that's true. But if it is, then I'd say the other 20% is the most important. Simply showing up and watching TV on a treadmill – that's not enough. Your greatest opportunity is to use your time in a way that will garner the most productive return. To take risks that will shake things up.

What can you do, right now, that would be the most powerful use of this moment?

EPILOGUE

I am grateful to you.

I want to live in a world in which each of us can show up, fully, as ourselves, every day, with confidence, connection, commitment, and courage. It would be a world in which we listen without getting defensive, and speak our truth with clarity and compassion. A world in which we take risks to pursue the things that are important to us and do it so well, so inspiringly, that others are clamoring to get on board.

I want to live in a world in which we take chances and fail and get up again. A world in which we understand – or at least consider – what's important enough to do, that we are willing to fail in pursuit of it. I want us to feel our own emotions deeply and become comfortable sitting with other people's emotions – even if that means experiencing anger directed at us. I want us to experience rising above our emotions – not repressing them – but acting deliberately while fully feeling them – to do things we know are right even if we are afraid or uncertain. And I want that to engender a deep trust in ourselves and in the people around us.

I want us to be real human beings – with cracks and challenges and emotions – and to stand strong as leaders, to move forward with what is important to us, not despite our humanness but because of it.

That's the world in which I want to live. Those are the people with whom I want to work and lead. And this is the book that I hope will help make that happen.

Thank you for joining me in this journey.

ACKNOWLEDGMENTS

This book would not exist without everything I have learned from Ann Bradney, who introduced me to the idea, importance, skill, and personal example of feeling everything. Thank you, Ann, for your leadership, for pouring your soul into creating the Radical Aliveness Institute (RAI), for your tremendous emotional courage, and for your deep commitment to creating a world in which more of us have more of it. And thank you to my classmates, fellow students, and teachers at RAI for supporting me, challenging me, and learning with me.

Jessica Gelson, my friend forever, your belief in me nourishes my belief in myself. Our work together creating the Leadership Intensive is so foundational, not only to this book, but to who I am and who I am becoming. In fact, ever since we met as teenagers, you have been foundational to who I am and who I am becoming. I am so grateful for our friendship and our work together.

Emily Cohen, I am so grateful that we get to work together every day, that you are so skilled and dedicated to honing the ideas in this book, and that you make emotional courage concrete in our coaching and with our clients. Thank you for your tireless commitment to excellence, integrity, and empathy. Thank you for caring so deeply. Thank you for your leadership and for your friendship.

Howie Jacobson, your friendship continues to be a source of strength for me, and our early conversation about how feelings are at the root of all action (and inaction) was one of the important seeds that grew into this book. Thank you.

Thank you to all the amazing leaders who have come to the Bregman Leadership Intensive, many of you more than once. Thank you for risking everything to find your ground, connect with each other, and build your capacity to inspire action on your most important work. You were on my mind every minute I was writing. You inspire me.

At Bregman Partners, I am blessed to be surrounded by an amazing group of coaches who inspire our clients, one another, and me every day. To those of you who work with us, and to those who have come to our trainings, thank you for showing up with your own emotional courage and for leading with confidence, connection, and commitment.

I am so thankful to our clients who are living this book every day. Strategy execution – having hard conversations, creating accountability, and inspiring focused action on your most important work – *is* the hard work of leadership, requiring all four elements. Thank you for partnering with us, for trusting us, and for going to uncomfortable places in the service of achieving your ambitious goals.

Thank you Anahid Avsharian, Clare Marshall, and Ryan Cadigan for making sure that what we present to the world is clear, powerful, and professional. You make me proud of everything we do.

Thank you Jim Levine for your belief in me and my work and for standing behind it so completely. You are the very best agent an author could ask for. Thank you Richard Narramore, and your team at Wiley, for loving this book and making it real and beautiful, and doing it so gracefully. The book is so much better for your efforts!

Thank you to my parents, Mama and Papa, whom I must thank every time I get the opportunity, never out of obligation, always from deep love and appreciation for how truly lucky I am to have been born your son.

Finally, and most especially, Eleanor, and the children we love so much, Isabelle, Sophia, and Daniel. You are all over this book, both in words, and in energy. You are my teachers, my comfort, my guides, my challengers, my everything. I love you more than words can say.

ABOUT THE AUTHOR

Peter Bregman is the founder and CEO of Bregman Partners, Inc., a company that helps organizations create aligned, committed, and collaborative teams that effectively execute their strategy and get their organization's most important work done.

For over 20 years, Peter has worked with CEOs and senior executives to help them identify and address the critical leadership and organizational gaps that are getting in the way of executing and achieving their strategic vision. He helps leaders develop their leadership skills, build aligned, collaborative teams, and overcome obstacles to drive results for their organizations.

Peter, an Inc.com Top 100 Leadership Speaker, is a sought-after speaker and thought leader in the areas of leadership development, organizational change, productivity, and emotional courage. He is a regular contributor to the *Harvard Business Review*, and his articles and commentary appear frequently in *Bloomberg BusinessWeek*, *Fast Company*, *Psychology Today*, *Forbes*, *The Financial Times*, PBS, ABC, CNN, NPR, and FOX Business News. He is also the host of the *Bregman Leadership Podcast*, which offers insightful conversations with industry thought leaders on how to become more powerful, courageous leaders. Peter is the author of *18 Minutes: Find Your Focus, Master Distraction, and Get the Right Things Done*, a *Wall Street Journal* bestseller, winner of the Gold medal from the Axiom Business Book awards, named the best business book of the year on NPR, and selected by *Publisher's*

Weekly and the *New York Post* as a top-10 business book. He also wrote *Four Seconds: All the Time You Need to Replace Counter-Productive Habits with Ones That Really Work*, a *New York Post* top pick for your career in 2015, and *Point B: A Short Guide to Leading a Big Change,* and is a contributor to six other books.

Peter earned his BA from Princeton University and his MBA from Columbia University. He can be reached at peter@bregmanpartners.com.